CW01512647

Wonder
No
More

The Endless Debate Has Ended

Bob Morley

Wonder No More

© 2011 Bob Morley
All rights reserved

Printed in the United States of America

Unless otherwise noted Scriptures are from the HOLY BIBLE:
NEW INTERNATIONAL VERSION. 1973, 1978, 1984 by International Bible Society. Used by permission of
Zondervan Publishing House. All rights reserved.

Scriptures marked kjv are from the Holy Bible, King James Version

Copyright: 2011
U.S. Library of Congress
TXu 1-569-861

Revised: 2016

Dedication

This book is dedicated
to my sister, Sharon.
I love you, Sis.

Chapter One

So, once in a while you wonder if there is a god who made everything. Welcome to the human race. Almost everyone wonders that same thing from time to time. And that includes most of the folks who grew up believing in a divine creator. The subject has been the hot topic of debate since man first sat around the campfire outside his cave. The strange thing is that after all of those thousands of years, and probable millions of discussions and debates, no one has ended that debate with definitive proof that either God is or He isn't.

According to the World Almanac and Encyclopedia Britannica we have over ten thousand religions in the world today, including atheism, so it would seem that at least one of them could have come up with something that would let us know for sure one way or another. But the maddening response from all of them involves taking what they say by faith. Personally, I would like a little more evidence than that. And I'll bet you would, too.

We would think that if a person or thing was smart enough to create everything, he or she would be smart enough to show us that he or she is there. But how could he do that? Obviously, in order to create us he would need to be outside our dimension, outside our time and space. That being the case, we could not possibly see him. Atheists point to the fact that we can't see a god as one of their main reasons for believing that there is no god. And since we can never see him, because if he created us he is in a different dimension, all we could ever see would be what he created within our own dimension.

On first thought, being able to see what was created should be enough to prove that at least there was a creator. It was definitely good enough for humans prior to the advent of the scientific era. But since science needs to be able to duplicate something to call it provable, divine creation to the scientist is only a theory. Of course, so is evolution. Neither one can be duplicated. Science can almost take us back in time to the "Big Bang," but that is like striking a match and "poof" there is fire. The big bang is the fire on the match, but who struck the match? Although it might seem to be common sense to think that someone had to strike that match, which we call "First Cause," we still do not have the proof we might need to conclude that there is in fact a god. To believe in creationism we are relegated to believing by faith alone.

And even though we are presented with evolution as if it were fact, the simple truth is that as the scientifically highly revered and die hard supporter of evolution, T.L. Moor, actually wrote,

4

"The more one studies paleontology, the more certain one becomes that **evolution is based on faith alone**." In other words, unfortunately neither evolution nor creationism are anything more at this point in time than unprovable theories. Neither theory truly proves anything with regard to whether a god does or does not exist. And so we wonder.

Let's pretend for a moment then that we were that creator, the person who struck the match that we now call the big bang. We've created a universe with all sorts of things in it, including people. Is there a way that we could let those people in on the fact that we exist? Remember, we are outside their time and space. They cannot see us, and never will be able to.

Maybe the key is the thing that seems to be the obstacle, being outside their time and space.

One of the very unique things someone who is outside of our time and space would be able to do is see people from their beginning all the way to their ending. Time, as people in the created universe would know it, would be nonexistent to someone outside of their dimension. In other words, if there were a god, He would be able to see the past and the future of all of mankind. He would have the super human advantage of being able to correctly predict what was going to happen each and every time, and never once be wrong. Only the creator of a new dimension would be able to do that. No one living in that dimension could ever come close to being accurate with predictions 100% of the time. But the creator would.

Therefore, to prove the existence of God all we have to do is find out if any gigantic body of predictions has been accurate 100% of the time. If we cannot find such a body of fulfilled predictions it will mean nothing. There may be no god, or there may be a god who just chooses not to tell us he is there. However, and this is the big one, if we **can** find that gigantic group of accurately fulfilled predictions, we will have found the illusive proof that God exists, and also that He wants to communicate with us.

Since we have over 10,000 religions in the world, we obviously have thousands of holy books. The logical place to begin our search, therefore, is in those books. However, let's confine our search to the holy books of the major religions: Buddhism, Judaism, Hinduism, Christianity, and Islam. And although we may find predictions, or as religions refer to them, prophecies, within those books, we need to be sure through historical record that the prophecies did indeed come true exactly as was prophesied. Showing a prophecy from the Koran or Bible as having been fulfilled within the Koran or Bible will do us no good without verifiable historical documentation.

Beyond that, it is logical that we should not use prophecies that were fulfilled within a hundred year time frame, to avoid any human tampering. For instance, if someone predicted that a person named Jacques Gibrandt would be ruler of France three hundred years from now, and that he would release a group of prisoners who had been found guilty of treason, after they had served exactly sixteen years in prison, and then if it were to become a fulfilled prediction, we would be impressed enough with that to let it be on our list.

Finally, we should make absolutely sure that the body of evidence, the group of fulfilled prophecies, far exceeds any chance of random occurrence. Predicting ten complicated future occurrences such as the one about Jacques Gibrandt, that are made over one hundred years in advance and historically documented as having been exactly fulfilled, should qualify as being beyond human capability. But let's go beyond that and say that in order for the predictor to be considered beyond our time and space he must accurately predict over **three hundred** of such complicated occurrences in a row and never once make a mistake. In other words, he must prove himself to us to be completely infallible. Only then will we be sure that we are dealing with someone outside of our dimension. As to whether he is the creator of everything, we will still need to know even more than that to be able to say that we have undeniable proof.

Ok. The ground rules have been laid out. Although we could start with the Jewish Torah, the Islamic Koran, the Hindu Veda, or any of the other holy books, let's take them in alphabetical order, starting with a prophecy from the Bible. We will do that in chapter two. We will go then to fulfilled prophecies from each of the other holy books in alphabetical order in following chapters and see what we can find. It should make for an interesting exercise. In fact, we could find God.

Chapter Two

Let's start with a prophecy from the Bible that even boldly told the name of one of the future prophetic participants, more than a hundred years before he was even born, even before his parents knew what they would name him, or even before they existed themselves. This fulfilled prophecy obviously caused the knees to wobble of the man it happened to when he found that he had been singled out by name in a hundred and fifty year old prophecy. I'll bet he shuddered at night for quite a few months after that.

We need to go back twenty six hundred years to find a fellow named Cyrus. His father, Cambyses, was king of Persia, while his mother, Mandane, was the daughter of the Median King Astgag. When Cambyses died in 559 BC, Cyrus took over the throne and became the Persian king. Not satisfied with just being the Persian king, he revolted against his Median grandfather and took over the Medes as well, thus uniting the Persian Mede Empire.

Conquest seemed to be Cyrus's calling, so he fairly quickly set out to conquer Asia Minor and Lydia as well. By 540 BC Cyrus decided that about the only thing left to add to his trophy case was Babylon. As long as Nebuchadnezzar had been the king of the Assyrians, Cyrus stayed put, but by 539

BC the feared king Nebuchadnezzar was dead and buried, and the likelihood of victory seemed easier. Nebuchadnezzar's son, Belshazzar, was in his second year at the Assyrian helm, so Cyrus marched his army straight to the Babylonia stronghold. Without us looking into the phenomenal "hand writing on the wall" episode, we'll just shorten the story by saying that without a single Medo-Persian loss of life, Cyrus put an end to the Assyrian Empire.

One of the things Cyrus did as king of pretty much the entire known world was free the Jewish slaves he found in Babylon. He did this in the spring of 536 BC. We know this not only because the Bible tells us, but because in 1880 an archaeologist named Hormuad Rassam excavated a cylinder which is now known as the Cyrus Cylinder, on which is written his conquests, as well as his policy to let the Israelite slave nation go home and rebuild their destroyed city of Jerusalem, as well as the temple to their God. This entire era is well documented in secular history. And the tomb of Cyrus, by the way, is still on the sightseeing 'things to see' list in the town of Pasargadae, Iran. This is obviously the type of historic documentation that we said in Chapter One that we would need before we could put any prophecy on our list.

Before we get into the really juicy part, let me mention that the reason the Jews were being held in captivity in the first place was that Nebuchadnezzar and his ferocious Assyrians had pretty much wiped out the nations of Israel and Judah back in the spring of 606 BC. We might mention that it was at that time that Daniel, of the later 'lion den' fame, was taken into captivity. By the time Cyrus showed up, Daniel was an old man of.

Over a hundred years before Cyrus was even born, about 700 BC, the Bible prophesied in Isaiah 45:1-5, *"This is what the Lord says to His anointed, to Cyrus, whose right hand I take hold of to subdue nations before him and to strip kings of their armor, to open doors before him so that gates will not be shut: I will go before you and will level the mountains; I will break down the gates of bronze and cut through the bars of iron. I will give you the treasures of darkness, riches stored in secret places, so that you may know that I am the Lord, the God of Israel, who summons you by name. For the sake of Jacob my servant, of Israel my chosen, I summon you by name and bestow on you a title of honor, though you do not acknowledge me. I am the Lord, and there is no other; apart from me there is no God."*

In the chapter preceding that in the Bible we read, *"This is what the Lord says - your redeemer, who formed you in the womb: . . . who says of Cyrus, 'He is my shepherd and I will accomplish all I please; he will say of Jerusalem, 'Let it be rebuilt,' and of the temple, 'let its foundations be laid."*

Isaiah 44:24-28.

11

Think long and hard about what we just read. Well over a hundred years before Cyrus was even born, and almost a hundred years before the Jewish people were even overthrown by the Assyrians, we find a message in the Bible that tells you and me that there would form a baby in its mother's womb who would be named Cyrus. This child would later become a mighty enough king to take over the fierce Assyrians, during a future Israelite captivity that had not even begun. The Biblical prophecy then foretold that Cyrus would also free the enslaved Jews and let them rebuild their capital city and its temple, both of which were still standing at the time the prophecy was written.

As we discussed, only someone outside of our time and space could predict such a series of events that would come true a hundred and fifty years later. Obviously no human could do something like that.

As an aside, the famous historian, Josephus, tells us that Cyrus was actually handed the scroll of Isaiah in which God had written His letter to him. We can be confident that the fact that the Jewish God had talked directly to him so many years in advance was the reason that Cyrus readily freed the Jewish slaves and allowed them to return to Jerusalem and rebuild their city and temple. Interestingly, however, Cyrus never stopped his pagan worship, just as was foretold in Isaiah, when the Lord said to the then unborn Cyrus, *"though you do not acknowledge me."*

Let's examine this historic episode deeper. In 700 BC the nations of Israel and Judah were doing fine. They were in such good shape that they had totally thrown their God out of their society and were head over heels into the worship of idols. They thought that they were invincible. They thought that they had no need for the God of their forefathers, a God they could not see.

It was foretold in numerous books of the Bible that the Jewish God had had enough of their idol worship. It was told to them in several prophecies that they were going into captivity for their refusal to acknowledge their God. In fact, through His prophet Jeremiah, God had told them, *"And this land shall be a desolation and astonishment and these nations shall serve the king of Babylon seventy years."* Jeremiah 25:11.

Did you notice that not only did the prophecy tell them that they were going into captivity, but it also told them what country would defeat them, and for how long the captivity would last? That in itself is an astonishing prophecy that was fulfilled exactly as the Bible said it would be.

Obviously the prophecies were right about the defeating king being the Assyrian king who reigned from Babylon. Now, let's add up the years and see about the seventy year part. From the spring of 606 BC to the spring of 536 BC is exactly seventy years. Astonishing!

Here we are at just the beginning of our study and it is fairly obvious already that there might truly be someone outside of our limited dimension.

Chapter Three

We have seen in the story of Cyrus from the Bible that there could be someone from outside our time and space that foresaw the future enough to make a totally accurate prediction of a complicated event, well over a hundred years in advance. And the fact that the actual event was documented historically outside of the Bible also meets the criteria we set up in Chapter One to try and find proof for the existence of God. But although there were really several fulfilled prophecies in that one story, let's continue on and see what size body of predictions we can find.

Before we leave the Bible to dig into the prophecies contained within the Islamic Koran, the Hindu Veda, and the Buddhist Dhammapada, I think it would be wise to check out one other interesting prophecy from the Bible that was fulfilled less than seventy years ago. It is a complicated one, but fun to unravel.

One of the people who lived during the period of captivity that we discussed in the last chapter was Ezekiel. An interesting thing about him is that poor Ezekiel often had to act out the prophecies in order to have a more dramatic effect on the Jews who were around him. For instance, Ezekiel was once told to lie on his left side for 390 days, and then on his right side for an additional 40 days. Ezekiel was told that this was to represent punishment for Israel's disobedience. These antics surely must have caused his friends to take notice.

The exact instruction to Ezekiel was, *"I have assigned you the same number of days as the years of their sin. So for 390 days you will bear the sin of the house of Israel. After you have finished this, lie down again, this time on your right side, and bear the sin of the house of Judah. I have assigned you 40 days, a day for each year."* Ezekiel 4:5-6.

The Bible goes on to tell the people of Israel through the prophet, Ezekiel, that their God is extremely angry with them because they've been worshiping idols instead of Him. That, of course, is the reason for their current bondage in Babylon. Their God then explains His future punishment by saying, *"I will inflict punishment on you and will scatter your survivors to the winds."* Ezekiel 5:10.

So, what we know at this point is that because of the Jewish infidelity to their God, He is going to punish them for a total period of 430 years (390 years for the sins of Israel, plus 40 years for the sins of Judah), and that their 430 year punishment will include a period of captivity, plus a period of being scattered to the winds.

We also know from what we learned in the last chapter that the captivity lasted seventy years, exactly as the Bible also had predicted. Logic tells

16

us that the Jews were going to be in for a period of 360 years of being scattered after the slavery in Babylon was over. That is the total of 430 years minus the 70 years of captive punishment already served. On top of that, we know that the captivity ended in 536 BC when Cyrus released the Jews to return to their promised land to rebuild Jerusalem and their temple.

We need to also know, though, that history tells us that only about 42,000 of the half million population of Jews in Babylon actually made the 600 mile journey back to Jerusalem. Most of the rest decided to just stick around in Babylon. Actually, that makes sense. We must realize that after 70 years in captivity the vast majority of released Jews did not even remember their parents' old land. It stands to reason when we consider that after the Civil War very few released slaves made any effort to return to Africa either. By that time, America was home. It was the only home they really knew.

Other than the 42,000 Jews who headed back to Jerusalem, the ones who did want to pick up their few belongings and start life anew decided to go north to lands they had heard about that sounded like more prosperous territory. Additionally, of the 42,000 who did return to their parents' homeland, very few could be called true children of God. Most of those 42,000 had long since been indoctrinated to the worship of pagan Babylonian idols, and they continued to worship those idols in Jerusalem.

Getting back to our prophecy, it should be obvious that since the Bible had said that the total period of punishment would be 430 years, and since the 70 years in captivity had already been served, we should now see the nation of Israel come back together 360 years later, which would be 176 BC. That was the predicted year for the end of the total punishment, the end of the scattering to the winds. This is where the story really gets fun, because in 176 BC nothing happened. The scattering of the Jews just got wider and wider.

The fact is that as scholars came and went through the centuries trying to make some sense of this prophecy gone awry, the only answer that seemed to fit was a type of debaters' answer that there "really was no answer." People needed to either just "keep the faith and believe" in the face of this doubt, or jump up and down and say, "We've got you, there is no god." Century after century dragged on this way. No one could figure out why the "scattering of Israel" did not end in 176 BC. The Jews kept getting scattered farther and farther apart. They were constantly thrown out of nations, or persecuted unmercifully in places like Russia and Hitler's Germany.

The ingathering never occurred. They even lost their native language, Hebrew, which basically became a dead language like Latin. The scattered Jewish people found themselves in 70 different nations, hated by almost everyone.

It seemed like the Bible had really goofed up this time. There was even the famous prophecy of God showing Ezekiel the valley of dry bones, symbolizing the nation of Israel. In that story God asked, *"Can these bones live?"* He then told Ezekiel, *"Prophesy to these bones and say to them, 'dry bones, hear the word of the Lord! This is what the sovereign Lord says to these bones: I will make breath enter you, and you will come to life. I will attach tendons to you and make flesh come upon you and cover you with skin; I will put breath in you and you will come to life. Then you will know that I am the Lord."* Ezekiel 37:3.

God even boldly went on to say in verse 20, *"I will take the Israelites out of the nations where they have gone. I will gather them from all around and bring them back into their own land. I will make them one nation in the land, on the mountains of Israel."*

Later, to another one of His favorite people, God had the audacity to tell the whole world, including you and me, that this rebirth would happen in only one day. Isaiah was told to write down,

"Who has ever heard such a thing? Who has ever seen such a thing? Can a country be born in one day or a nation be brought forth in a moment? ...Rejoice with Jerusalem and be glad for her, all you who love her, rejoice greatly with her, all you who mourn over her." Isaiah 66:8-9.

19

After time seemed to drag endlessly on, scholars began to write books about how the Jews would be reunited again as prophesied, but that it would happen in heaven. It seemed impossible that this prophecy could ever be fulfilled on earth, but they did not admit to the public that their God had made a mistake.

Poor Ezekiel's having to lie on his sides for a total of 430 days was brushed aside and tried to be forgotten as the blunder that it obviously was. No one wanted to talk about it at all. It was a mystery sent to the closet of "faith".

Then, like a whirlwind, events took place almost in an instant on the real life historical stage. On May 15, 1948, Israel once again became a nation, in one day. Everything happened as predicted. The Bible was given more credence. Everything happened the way it said it would happen.

The problem for everyone "in the know" was that everything really didn't happen the way the Bible said it would. The astute Bible scholars deep down inside knew that the prophecy had predicted it would happen in 176 BC. A day or two off would have been one thing, but a prophetic miss of over two thousand years is a stretch by anybody's rules. If this prophetic date was wrong, the very existence of an all knowing God could well be in question.

Enter now an extremely smart student of the Bible named Dr. Grant Jeffrey. For some reason he happened to notice a neglected fact that in Leviticus 26 the God of the Jews repeated a principle four separate times. In verse 18 He said, *"If after all this you will not listen to me, I will punish you for your sins seven times over."* God went on to reiterate the point in verse 21 by saying, *"If you remain hostile to me and refuse to listen to me, I will multiply your afflictions seven times over, as your sins deserve."*

The Israelites evidently were like children and had to be warned over and over, so in the same chapter, verses 23 & 24, the promise was reworded again by saying, *"If in spite of these things you do not accept my correction but continue to be hostile toward me, I myself will be hostile to you and will inflict you for your sins seven times over."* And just for good measure God drove home the point in verse 28 with, *"Then in my anger I will be hostile toward you, and I myself will punish you for your sins seven times over."*

All right, it now seems fairly clear that if God pronounced a punishment, and the attitude adjustment He required did not occur, His children were going to sit in the corner seven times longer than He originally had specified.

So let's review what had happened. God had told the Jewish people that because they did not acknowledge Him as God, they were going to have 430 years of punishment, including 70 years as slaves to the Babylonians, plus 360 years of being scattered to the wind. That should have all occurred from 606 BC to 176 BC. The rub was that after the first seventy years the Jews were supposed to realize that He was their God and repent. Unfortunately, that didn't happen. Even the few who returned to Jerusalem snubbed the majority of their 42,000 noses at Him. They either continued worshiping the idols they had worshiped in Babylon, or they worshiped nothing.

Now, though, knowing the seven times rule, we can look back and see if God's prophecy of time was correct after all. The first thing we need to do is multiply the remaining 360 years of punishment left after the captivity by seven. That gives us 2,520 years. Next we need to convert from the 360 day years of the Hebrew lunar calendar to our years which contain 365 1/4 days. That means that the new punishment period of scattering for the Jews should last 2,484 of our solar years. Hang in there. We are just about finished doing math.

So, counting 2,484 years from 536 BC forward, we come up to the year 1948. Even more astonishing than the year is the fact that if we take the total number of days involved, 907,200, and move forward from the date of Cyrus's decree, which we do know, we end up at May 15, 1948. That is the exact date that Israel declared itself as a nation and was accepted by the UN, the only time in the history of the world that a nation actually became a nation in only one day, exactly as God said would happen in Isaiah 66:8, to the exact day.

Over 2,500 years in advance, God predicted the exact date that Israel would again become a nation, and on May 15, 1948, it happened exactly as He said it would.

Surely only someone outside of our time dimension could have pulled this one off. Can any man or woman alive actually debate with a straight face the fact that there is a creator in the face of such an astonishing plethora of amazing predictions? It would be unfathomable, but there is even more, as we shall soon see.

Chapter Four

We obviously have made quite a bit of progress already in determining if God exists. But let's leave the Bible and look at a few of the many other holy books and see how many fulfilled prophecies we might find in them as well. The next book in alphabetical order is the Dhammapada, one of many holy books of Buddhism. Unfortunately, there is not one single fulfilled prophecy in this holy book. That might be a little surprising and disappointing, especially to Buddhists, but let's not get discouraged. Remember, there are thousands of holy books we can dig into to find more fulfilled prophecies that could come from God, outside our time and space.

Islam's holy book, the Koran, since it is studied so reverently by over a billion Muslim followers, surely will give us plenty of prophecies that we can check out. At least we would think so. The truth, however, is that like the Buddhist Dhammapada, the Islamic Koran contains not a single fulfilled prophecy. We would think that if it is true that Islam, Judaism, and Christianity all come from the same God, as most of the world seems to believe, there would certainly be a generous sprinkling of fulfilled prophecy in the Koran, like there is the Bible. But that is not the case. Although there is an abundance of fulfilled prophecies in the Bible, there is not even one in the Koran. Not one.

Going further alphabetically to the Veda of Hinduism we find that the same thing is true. The Veda contains not a single fulfilled prophecy. In fact, an examination of every one of the thousands of holy books in the world reveals a startling, and telling, truth: the Bible, including the first five books within it which make up the Jewish Torah, is the only book of all of the thousands of holy books of all the 10,000 world religions that contains any fulfilled prophecies. It is obvious, therefore, that if indeed God exists, He chose to communicate to us through only one written source, the Holy Bible. All of the other holy books (with a lower case 'h'), must have been written by mere men, human beings like us who were limited to our dimension.

But getting back to our search, since we set up some initial guidelines, are there over three hundred fulfilled prophecies in the Holy Bible? The answer is an astonishing yes. Not only are there three hundred, but careful study of the Bible produces over **six thousand fulfilled prophetic verses**, each one just as amazing as the few we have already examined in Chapters Two and Three. In fact, every single Biblical prophecy that should have been fulfilled by now, has wonderfully been fulfilled, exactly as predicted.

Think about what you just read. It may well be the most important paragraph you have ever read, or will ever read. In actuality it may be the most important paragraph ever written. In that paragraph is the truth that the Holy Bible contains over six thousand prophetic verses that should have been fulfilled by this point in time, and every single one of those six thousand has phenomenally been fulfilled exactly as it was predicted. Not one Biblical prophecy that should have been fulfilled has not been fulfilled. A whopping six thousand of them. This could not have happened by humans. Only someone outside our dimension, outside our time and space, could accurately predict future events hundreds, and often thousands of years in advance and never miss. Not one miss in six thousand far and away removes any possibility that anyone other than a being that can see all of time from the beginning of time to the end of time was responsible. No matter what anyone might try to say to rationalize this incredible fact, there is no other possibility. The source of the Holy Bible, and only the Holy Bible, is outside of human time and space. This source is in a totally different dimension than we are.

But what is the source? Who is this entity or person who is in a different dimension from the one we live in, and who is communicating with us. The simple fact is that for over 2,500 years the answer has been right under everyone's nose, but it seems that no one was paying attention. That source, that entity, that person, told us Himself who He is. That incredible, supernatural person who gave us over six thousand prophetic verses in the Holy Bible that all have been fulfilled exactly as they were supposed to be told us, *"I am God, and there is none like me. I make known the end from the beginning, from ancient times, what is still to come."* Isaiah 46:10.

That is probably one of the two or three most important verses in the entire Bible and most people in history completely skipped over it. That one piece of communication from outside our time and space explained very simply how all of mankind could know for a certainty that God exists. But idiotic mankind chose to participate in an inanely ridiculous debate for thousands of years. Instead of heeding the divine words of our Creator, the entire human race decided that the only way to believe in God was to take His existence by faith. God must have been wondering Himself, but in His case He must have been wondering what kind of idiots He had created. He must have been shaking His head for millennia wondering when we were going to take Him at His word and look for the six thousand proofs He gave us that He exists.

While we were wondering if God exists, He has been wondering if we would ever wake up from our moronic stupor. I say that tongue in cheek, knowing that He knows *"the end from the beginning,"* so He knew that this book would eventually be written and published and that your eyes and mine would be opened to the provable reality that God exists.

Of course, while waiting for this information to come to light, mankind has come up with some of the silliest things imaginable, such as worshipping created things like trees, the sun, the moon, or animals. Outlandishly, we even find religions today that believe that a man himself is or can be a god. I find it funny that God not only foresaw that egotistical stupidity happening, and being promoted in places like TV on the such things as The Oprah Winfrey Show, so He even threw out the gauntlet to anyone that thought they could predict future events like He could. God said to those who thought they could, *"Present your case,' the Lord God says. 'Bring forth your strong arguments,' the King of Jacob says. 'Let them declare to us what is going to take place; as for the former events, declare what they were, that we may consider them, and know their outcome; or announce to us what is coming. Declare the things that are going to come afterward, so that we may know that you are gods."* Isaiah 41:21-23 (NASB).

God told us plainly ***"I am God, and there is none like me. I make known the end from the beginning, from ancient times, what is still to come."*** Isaiah 46:10. In that extremely important verse He told us that there is *none* like Him. He is the only God. No man could ever become god. And for that matter, no other god of any other religion is a real god, not the Muslim Allah, not Buddha, not the Hindu sacred cows. There is one God, and one God only, the Judeo/Christian God of the Bible. The God who called Himself *"I am."*

But let's look at more astonishing proof. It is all in plain view for all mankind to examine. And it is truly spine tingling to see, once we finally realize that there is no other explanation for its existence than that it came from outside our time and space, from the One we often wondered or debated about, God, our Creator. God, the Great I Am.

Chapter Five

We have already seen in just a few illustrations that are startling to say the least, that the existence of God is undeniable. If you haven't come to that conclusion yet, I'm convinced that you will be as we examine a few more exciting examples of God's complete infallibility.

Some remarkable prophecies have to do with one of my boyhood heroes, Alexander the Great. For those of us who studied hard at the last minute for our high school and junior high history tests, and then promptly forgot every name and date the minute we laid our pencils down, it might be a good idea to first take a look at this young man who accomplished more in fifteen years than any other figure in history. In fact, he changed the world for the future more than anyone else who ever lived, with the exception, of course, of Jesus.

When Alexander was born in 356 BC, Greece was still just a geographical grouping of five different tribes who hated and were constantly at battle with each other. It was the Hatfields and McCoys times four. Skirmishes and outright battles were daily occurrences, and had been since long before anyone could remember. Each tribe had their own warrior king, and Alexander's father, Phillip, was the king of the tribal state of Macedonia.

Talk about an education, Alexander's teacher as a young lad was none other than the great Greek philosopher, Aristotle. If you have ever read works by Aristotle, you can appreciate why the young Alexander often would sneak away and run off to watch his father train his men for battle. That obviously was a lot more fun for a boy than listening to Aristotle hour after hour. And with these training exercises as a class room, Alexander was to become one of the military geniuses of all time.

At age eighteen Alexander's life, and the life of our planet, changed dramatically with the thrust of a knife by a lunatic assassin. Phillip was killed on the steps of the temple of Zeus and instantly our young hero became the king of Macedonia. Alexander, who was with his father at the time, did jump in and kill the assassin, but there has always been some speculation that possibly he had some part in the plot.

While watching his father train his army, Alexander had been formulating battle tactics in his mind. Now that he was king he quickly trained his inherited army in these revolutionary strategies, including a brand new battle formation he came up with known as the phalanx, which along with other ingenious new tactics, introduced the speed of a leopard to his fighting forces. Within just months he had indoctrinated his charges in these new maneuvers and he set out to conquer all four of the other Grecian tribes.

Not only did Alexander succeed with lightning fast speed to defeat the other armies, which no other Greek had ever been able to do, but he convinced the other tribes to unite and form one nation. His men loved him, partially because he never told them what to do in battle, but instead said only, "Follow me." His bravery and courage were never questioned. It is interesting that through the years literally thousands of arrows, lances, and swords came flying in his direction, but he did not die on the battle field. As we read on we will get a clue as to why.

One of the problems the brilliant young Alexander could immediately see with this new Greek nation was that each of the five former tribes spoke a different language. He understood that this would cause a gigantic communication problem, especially in battle, since his army would now be a combination of the previous five tribal armies. Having studied at Aristotle's feet, who himself was a master linguist, Alexander sat down and created, by himself, a new language from the different dialects. It was called Koine Greek, or common Greek, and he demanded that all his soldiers learn it.

In only two years Alexander felt that his new combined army was ready for conquest, and he personally hungered for it. As we saw a few chapters back, a few hundred years earlier Cyrus had united the Medes and the Persians and this new Medo-Persian empire, now led by King Darius, was in total control of most of the known world. Alexander wanted what Darius had. The problem was that his army, and brand new baby nation, did not share his confidence that the forces of Darius could be defeated.

Secretly Alexander decided to change that. Under the pretext of liberating the oppressed Greeks living in Troy, on the western coast of what is now Turkey, Alexander led his superiorly trained army against a few Medo-Persian outposts. He advertised it to his subjects as a quick in and out liberation raid. Unknown to all his advisers and generals, Alexander had two underlying motives.

He knew that he could raise his army's confidence with rapid victories, and he also knew that he would infuriate King Darius who would bring his entire might against him. That was what Alexander really wanted. He alone in Greece knew that his army could defeat Darius if it was forced to fight.

Like lightning the new Grecian army obliterated several smaller Medo-Persian outposts, which did indeed raise his army's spirits; and at the same time he positioned his own forces so that there would be no way for them to escape, should Darius join the fray with his whole force. His army would have to fight.

As planned, Darius was enraged and mobilized his formidable forces to teach this upstart Greek king a lesson. But Alexander had been planning for this for years as he would lie in his bed at night. The strategy he devised was to quickly demoralize the Persian army. And his plan to accomplish that was to immediately destroy their most elite battalion. With the cunning of a leopard Alexander actually stalked this battalion, and when he felt the terrain was perfect he led his entire force straight at them with his new phalanx maneuver, tearing them to shreds so quickly that even his own army didn't realize what had happened. The rest of the Medo-Persian army was completely stunned. They had never seen anything like this, and inside each of Darius's men was fear. The confidence now in the hearts of the Greeks was at an all-time high.

Alexander did not stop to rest on his laurels. He immediately kept up the offensive, picking and choosing his lightning swift attacks. The Medo-Persian army was in total disarray. The solders of Darius panicked and fled, leaving their king unprotected. In fact, two of those soldiers, seeking to gain favor with Alexander, killed King Darius and rushed to tell him. Alexander's response was that only a king could kill a king, and he immediately slew both of the traitors himself.

Alexander had done the impossible. He had defeated the army that supposedly could not be defeated. And he had done it almost effortlessly. His own army was delirious. This upstart nation that had been created almost overnight from a band of five rival tribes, that didn't even speak the same language, had demolished the greatest power in the world. The year was 331 BC, and Alexander was only 25 years old. From then on his soldiers would follow him to the gates of hell if he said, "Follow me."

Even though Alexander now was king over not only Greece, but the entire Medo-Persian Empire, he was not satisfied. He wanted the whole world. And basically that is what he got. His army headed south and took control of the land bridge that united the three continents of Asia, Africa, and Europe. This land bridge extended from Egypt in the south all the way north to what is now Istanbul, Turkey. They then even conquered land all the way eastward to India and the gateway to China.

Alexander was not just a military genius, though, because his ideas of winning over the conquered people were equally as effective as his military strategies. Once an empire or nation was under his control he did not enslave them. Instead, he allowed them to pretty much do things the way they wanted. His only real passion was that they embrace the Greek culture and his new "Common Greek" language. This practice endeared him to his subjects worldwide.

In 323 BC Alexander the Great died at the young age of 33. In fifteen short years he had conquered the known world. In the process he united the world in language in a way that even the Roman Empire that would come later could not change. Even the Israelites who were scattered around the world found that they needed to have their scriptures that we now call the Old Testament translated from Hebrew into Greek, in what is referred to as the Septuagint, or LXX. As an aside, the name Septuagint comes from the fact that it took seventy translators seven months to complete. And interestingly, the translation was done in the city that bears our hero's name, Alexandria, Egypt.

When Alexander died his son was at his side. This boy would normally have been given the scepter; however, when asked, "To whom do you will your kingdom?" he replied, "Give it to the strong." As a result, his four generals divided up the empire. Lysimachus took Greece. Cassander got Asia Minor. Seleucus took Syria and east to old Persia. And Ptolemy took Egypt and a big part of North Africa.

In fifteen short years Alexander had completely changed the face of the world and much of its future. Though many have tried, never before or after has there been anyone like him. He truly was "the Great."

So why in the world did we spend so much time in a history lesson on Alexander the Great? Because God told his story hundreds of years in advance through His prophet Daniel. In fact, when Alexander and his army headed south to conquer Egypt he naturally took over Jerusalem and the rest of Israel as well. History tells us that the high priest at the time requested an audience with Alexander and showed him the second, seventh, and eighth chapters of Daniel, in which God had foretold his life. Alexander is reputed to have fallen down and declared the God of Israel the God of gods. He then took with him many of the Jewish royal family of Judah and made them administrators of the conquered lands. This had much to do with the further scattering of the Jews and the need for the Septuagint to be printed in Alexander's own language.

Let's see exactly what God had said back during the time when Nebuchadnezzar's Assyrian Empire was at its zenith, before Cyrus had even united the Medes and Persians and created the empire that Alexander would later destroy. At the time these prophecies were made there was no nation of Greece, and the smartest people of the time would have wagered all they had on the probability that those five warring tribes that lived there could never be united, no less ever become world conquerors. But even hundreds of years in advance, God could see everything that would happen in the future.

The book of Daniel is one of the most phenomenal books in the Bible. The prophecies contained in it are so detailed that only someone outside our time limitations could have uttered them. The fulfilling of many of them occurred with our hero, Alexander, and his four generals, and you are going to be awe struck as you read them in the next chapter.

To give you just a taste, though, I will tell you that through Daniel, God was to outline a bit of future that we now can look at as history.

In these remarkable prophecies God outlined the four world empires; the Assyrians, the Persia-Medes, the Greeks, and the Romans; but let's take a quick glance at what God showed Daniel in two separate visions about Alexander.

About his first vision, Daniel said in chapter 8, "*Suddenly a goat with a prominent horn between his eyes came from the west, crossing the whole earth without touching the ground. He came toward the two horned ram I had seen standing beside the canal and charged at him in great rage. I saw him attack the ram furiously, striking the ram and shattering his two horns. The ram was powerless to stand against him; the goat knocked him to the ground and trampled on him, and none could rescue the ram from his power. The goat became very great, but at the height of his power his large horn was broken off, and in its place four prominent horns grew up toward the four winds of heaven,*"

God, being all wise, knew that debaters would come along who scoffed at this and said that it could have represented several people in history, or none at all. So, leaving nothing to chance, God sent an angel to Daniel to interpret the vision for him, and for us. Here is what the angel had to say in verses 20 through 22, "*The two horned ram that you saw represents the kings of Media and Persia. The shaggy goat is the king of Greece* (Remember, Greece was hundreds of years away from even becoming a nation at that time), *and the large horn between his eye is the first king* (The first king of Greece was Alexander). *The four horns that replaced the one that was broken off represent four kingdoms that will emerge from his nation but will never have the same power* (As we saw, Greece was divided among Alexander's four generals)."

To clarify it even more, God gave Daniel another dream and interpreted it as well through an angel in chapter 11. In the interpretation the angel says (speaking of Darius), *"When he has gained power by his wealth, he will stir up everyone against the kingdom of Greece. Then a mighty king will appear, who will rule with great power and do as he pleases. After he has appeared, his empire will be broken up and parceled out toward the four winds of heaven. It will not go to his descendants, nor will it have the power he exercised because his empire will be uprooted and given to others."*

Lest we forget, when Daniel was given these dreams, and these interpretations, the Assyrians under Nebuchadnezzar were the dominant world empire and Daniel was in captivity in the capital of Babylon, along with another Israelite we mentioned earlier by the name of Ezekiel. The thought of Greece becoming a united nation in the future would have been considered the ramblings of a lunatic. But God, of course, sees the whole future, and He showed Daniel what was going to happen, which fortunately provided us in the 21st century with unquestionable proof that He exists. He did not want that fact to become a "faith" issue. In the next chapter you will see the minutest details God would provide to make His point an unchallengeable one.

Chapter Six

I think you will see as we explore these next extremely detailed predictions, that the big reason for God going to the trouble of even having Daniel write them down probably was to establish to those of us living today that He does in fact exist. Hold on to your hat because what you are about to read is truly mind boggling.

I am just going to relate event by event as found in Daniel eleven. I think the best way to do that will be to quote a verse that foretold something, and then immediately tell you what actually happened. You will be fascinated as you read these comparisons. And, as you read them, remember to stay focused on the fact that each verse was written hundreds of years before the people involved were even born. Otherwise you will be trapped into thinking that what you are reading is a reporter's account of an event that happened the day before he wrote it. These fulfilled prophecies are that close to the way history actually played out. As I begin to write these comparisons I am absolutely convinced that you are going to be flabbergasted.

As you recall, when we left Alexander on his deathbed he had given his empire to the strong, which turned out to be his four generals. Again, Lysimachus took over the northern part, Cassander took Asia Minor, Seleucus took what is now Syria, and Ptolemy took the southern part of Egypt and parts of Africa.

We already read what the angel told Daniel in chapter eleven, would happen at Alexander's death, *"his empire will be broken up and parceled out toward the four winds. It will not go to his descendants, nor will it have the power he exercised, because the empire will be uprooted and given to others."*

Now we will continue in verse 5 of chapter eleven as the angel is describing what is going to happen afterwards. *"The king of the South will become strong, but one of his commanders will become stronger than he and will rule his own kingdom with great power."*

The king of the South was Ptolemy I, who took Egypt. Seleucus, who took Syria, had originally been a commander under Ptolemy in Alexander's army. Seleucus became the most powerful of the four new kings.

In verse 6 the angel continues, *"After some years they will become allies. The daughter of the king of the South will go to the king of the North to make an alliance, but she will not retain her power, and he and his power will not last. In those days she will be handed over with her royal escort and her father and the one who supported her."*

In that verse the phrase "after some years" is a term usually referring to the passing of a generation, which was the case here as well. In the next generation Ptolemy II is the king of the South and Antiochus II is the king of the North. Ptolemy II, in order to form an alliance, took his daughter, Berenice, to Syria to marry Antiochus II. Unfortunately they did not count on the wrath of a woman scorned, for Laodice, a former wife of Antiochus II had both Berenice and Antiochus II murdered. At the same time her father, Ptolemy II died somewhat mysteriously. For fun, go back and reread that verse. The detail is phenomenal.

Verses 7 through 9 tell us, *"One of her family line will arise to take her place. He will attack the forces of the king of the North and enter his fortress; he will fight against them and be victorious. He will also seize their gods, their metal images, and their valuable articles of silver and gold and carry them off to Egypt. For some years he will leave the king of the North alone. Then the king of the north will invade the realm of the king of the South but will retreat to his own country."*

Berenice's brother, Ptolemy III, invaded the North and won a great victory. With the spoils he brought back, he erected a big monument, called Marmor Adulitanum, in celebration of his victory. After that he left the North alone. In 240 BC the North invaded the South, led by Seleucus II, but the attack failed and the northern army went home like a dog with its tail between its legs. Once again, every detail came true. Reread it and see for yourself. Each verse is a WOW verse.

God's prophecy continues in verse 10 with, *"His sons will prepare for war and assemble a great army, which will sweep on like an irresistible flood and carry the battle as far as his fortress."*

Sure enough, the sons of Seleucus II, created a gigantic army. The older son, Seleucus III, was killed in battle in Asia Minor, but the younger son, Antiochus III, took the army like a flood all the way to the gates of Egypt and had some success before returning home.

In verse 11 we find prophetically, *"Then the king of the South will march out in rage and fight against the king of the North, who will raise a large army, but it will be defeated. When the army is carried off, the king of the South will be filled with pride and will slaughter many thousands,"*

Egypt's Ptolemy IV soundly defeated Antiochus III's 70,000 man army at the gigantic battle of Raphia. It was a complete destruction of the northern forces. God was 100% correct again, as always.

The prophecy goes on, *"yet he will not remain triumphant. For the king of the North will muster another army, larger than the first, and after several years, he will advance with a huge army fully equipped."*

Antiochus III could not get the Raphia defeat out of his mind, so fourteen years later he returned to Egypt with an even more massive army.

Verse 14 continues, *"In those times many will rise against the king of the South. The violent men among your own people will rebel in fulfillment of the vision, but without success."*

This is the first time in the eleventh chapter that the Hebrews are even mentioned, and as the above verse predicts, many Jews at this time did help Antiochus III against Egypt.

Hopefully you are keeping your focus where it needs to be in these verses. The events that are being described really happened about

200 BC, which is about three and a half centuries <u>after </u>the verses were actually written by Daniel.

Other than naming names as we saw He did with Cyrus, or prophesying the dates as He did with Israel's rebirth on May 15, 1948, what more could God have done to prove to us that He does exist, and that He exists without our time constraints? These verses are utterly awesome, so let's continue with the next verse, number 15.

"Then the king of the North will come and build up siege ramps and will capture a fortified city. The forces of the South will be powerless to resist; even their best troops will not have the strength to stand."

At this time Antiochus III captured the fortified city of Sidon in 198 BC. The Egyptians attempted to conquer Syria, but they were not able to do anything against the growing power of Antiochus III. The actual events and the prophesying verses continue to be startlingly identical.

In verse 16 we read, *"The invader will do as he pleases; no one will be able to stand against him. He will establish himself in the Beautiful Land and will have power to destroy it."*

As you can guess, by "Beautiful Land" God is referring to His holy land of Israel, and sure enough, Antiochus III next conquered Palestine.

The angel tells Daniel in the next verse, *"He will determine to come with the might of his entire kingdom and will make an alliance with the king of the South. And he will give him a daughter in marriage in order to overthrow the kingdom, but his plans will not succeed or help him."*

Antiochus now concocts a plan to have his daughter, Cleopatra marry Ptolemy V, hoping to take over a united kingdom. Cleopatra, however, had a mind of her own, and once married, sided with her new husband. This put the kibosh on poor old Antiochus's carefully planned out plot. If he had read God's Word in Daniel he would have known it would not work.

God's prophecy continues in verse 18, *"Then he will turn his attention to the coastlands and will take many of them, but a commander will put an end to his insolence and will turn his insolence back upon him. After this, he will turn back toward the fortresses of his own country but will stumble and fall, to be seen no more."*

Finally, Antiochus III decided to try to take control of Greece, but he was defeated in

191 BC at Thermopylae, and again two years later at Magnesia, southwest of Ephesus. The latter defeat was at the hands of the Romans. This last defeat crushed his spirit and he headed home, only to be killed along the way as he tried to plunder a temple at Elam.

Can you imagine being a Hebrew student of scripture at that time? You would not have needed to watch the evening news on TV, except to check off the events foretold in Daniel eleven as they occurred in the world around you. I'm confident that the reason God did not prophesy the exact dates, as He did elsewhere, was because He did not want the prophecies to interfere with the future events. He foretold them solely to prove to his people, and to us, that He was who He said He was, the God of all creation.

So let's explore the rest of this remarkable chapter, which in reality is an encapsulated history of the Grecian and Roman empires. I will mention before we go on that the Book of Daniel was actually a look at all of world history up to and including the time that we know as the "end times". But the purpose of these pages is not an examination of the fascinating end time prophecies, but the ones already fulfilled.

Chapter eleven of Daniel continues after the death of Antiochus III with verse 20 stating, *"His successor will send out a tax collector to maintain the royal splendor. In a few years, however, he will be destroyed, yet not in anger or in battle."*

As we have seen, Rome now came on the scene, and the successor to Antiochus III, Seleucus IV, had to come up with a way to pay the new Roman Empire a thousand talents each and every year. In order not to harm *"the royal splendor,"* Seleucus IV appointed a man named Heliodorus to collect taxes. Within a few years Seleucus IV was killed with poison, by his own tax collector no less, *"not in anger or in battle."* I am very tempted, but I won't type any tax collector jokes here. But wouldn't this be the perfect time for one?

The angel of God goes on to describe future events to Daniel by saying, *"He will be succeeded by a contemptible person who has not been given the honor of royalty. He will invade the kingdom when its people feel secure, and he will seize it through intrigue."*

When God said intrigue, He meant it. You may need a score card here. Seleucus IV's son,

Demetrius, was the logical successor to the throne, but he was in Rome in prison when his father overdosed on poison given to him by the tax man. The younger son was still a baby. Enter on the scene the brother of Seleucus IV, the conniving Antiochus IV.

Antiochus IV was in Athens when he heard of his brother's sudden departure. As God said, he was *"contemptible."* He got a friend of his in Antioch by the name of Andronicus to murder the young baby son of his brother Seleucus. After that terrible deed was done, Antiochus IV had Andronicus murdered.

He then succeeded in taking over his brother's business. As I said, talk about intrigue, this episode had plenty of it. And as usual, God hit the nail on the head every step of the way, hundreds of years in advance.

The adventures of Antiochus IV are the final ones we will look at in chapter eleven. Daniel's writing continues about him, *"Then an overwhelming army will be swept away before him."*

Almost immediately after Antiochus IV took power, Egypt sent a gigantic army to defeat him, but somehow the forces of Antiochus were able to repel them. At this point there are several more verses dealing with different back and forth battles with Egypt that did occur exactly as predicted.

Skipping down to verse 27, though, we read, *"The two kings, with their hearts bent on evil, will sit at the same table and lie to each other, but to no avail, because an end will still come at the appointed time."*

This attempted peace meeting did occur; however, in the end it was futile.

Verse 28 states, *"The king of the North will return to his own country with great wealth, but his heart will be set against the holy covenant. He will take action against it and then return to his own country."*

On his way back home from the failed peace talks with Egypt, Antiochus IV decided to plunder Jerusalem, which he did. In the process he killed 80,000 Hebrews and took another 40,000 into slavery.

The prophecy continues in verse 28 with, *"At the appointed time he will invade the South again, but this time the outcome will be different from what it was before. Ships from the western coastlands will oppose him and he will lose heart."*

Still obsessed with the desire to finally defeat Egypt once and for all, Antiochus IV heads back south with his army. This time, though, the Roman fleet *"from the western coastlands"* comes into the picture and he wisely decides that he had better give up his quest for good.

The final verses we will look at are verses 30 through 32, in which God lets Daniel see, *"Then he will turn back and vent his fury against the holy covenant. He will return and show favor to those who forsake the holy covenant. His armed forces will rise up to desecrate the temple fortress and will abolish the daily sacrifice. Then they will set up the abomination that causes desolation. But the people who know their God will firmly resist him."*

Antiochus IV took the loss of his goal to conquer Egypt out on the Israelites, partly because he blamed them for not fully supporting his endeavor, and partly because he simply hated the Jewish religion. He and his troops went into Jerusalem and completely desecrated the temple. He then even sacrificed a sow on the alter, which was a complete abomination, and even set up a statue of a Greek god in the holy place. This started a revolt that we know of as the Maccabean Revolt by thousands of religious Jews, which resulted in terrible slaughter.

The eleventh chapter of Daniel is one of the most remarkable in the entire Bible. And the purpose of it is probably primarily to show anyone that there is no debate about God's existence. Obviously it is a human impossibility to see into the future at all, much less in such startling and awesome detail like what we just looked at.

There cannot even be any discussion about the fact that God exists. It is not a matter of faith. It is real. It has been proven. And just the same as the fact that whether we know about the law of gravity or not, it is still fact, the same is true of God. Whether man is knowledgeable about the conclusive proof that God exists or is totally in the dark, does not change the fact; God is real. He was at the beginning of creation. He is now. And He will be forever. Our little beliefs one way or the other have no impact on that fact. The debates have always been ridiculous. But we need wonder no more.

Remember, in Isaiah 46 God told us, *"I am God and there is none like me. I make known the end from the beginning, from ancient times, what is still to come."*

Chapter Seven

The incredible fact that there are over six thousand prophetic verses in the Bible that have already come to pass does indeed prove the existence of a non-human being outside of our time and space. And the fact that all of those six thousand verses are found in the Bible and nowhere else should make it crystal clear to any reasonable human that the other worldly being responsible for that massive amount of fulfilled predictions is in fact the God of the Bible. Interestingly, that same Bible contains about twenty five hundred additional prophetic verses that tell of future events that encompass what we refer to as the end times. If you are intrigued enough to want to look into what those verses predict, may I suggest that you read my first book, <u>Unlocking God's Secrets</u>, because that book looks at those future events with an extremely unique and exciting twist that is not found anywhere else. In that book you will also read many of the six thousand exciting fulfilled prophecies that we won't be able to explore in this extremely short book. Additionally, you will also learn the reason for all of creation, as well as the true meaning of life that has never before been explained.

One question you might be asking yourself about now is "Why are the Biblical prophecies not presented in a much more clear and straight forward manner?" It does seem like the prophetic event is almost hidden from us as we read the prophecy. The prediction that Israel would become a nation on May 15. 1948, was unquestionably obscured to the casual reader of the Bible. Think about it, Ezekiel had to lie on both sides for 430 days, which seems kind of ridiculous. Then, even after the prediction was deciphered, it took twenty five hundred years before Dr. Grant Jeffrey came along and realized that the prediction had to be coupled with instructions found in a totally different Biblical book that was written about 800 years prior to the time of Ezekiel. It seems like, although God made the predictions, He tried to hide them from us. Is that strange, or what?

But let's ponder it. If God had just openly told us in the Bible that Israel would become a nation again on May 15, 1948, the vast majority of nations and peoples of the world who hated the Jews so passionately would have done everything in their power to prevent it. God did not want the knowledge of His prophecies to be used to alter coming world events. His reason for prophesying such a plethora of astounding predictions was for one reason only, to prove to us living today, beyond a shadow of a doubt, that He exists. That is why God gave them to us in such an obscure and complicated manner. Interestingly, God explained to us, *"It is the glory of God to conceal a matter; to search out a matter is the glory of kings."*

Proverbs 25:2.

There are, however, many tidbits of information that God did give mankind in a more straight forward manner that are similar to the prophetic verses in that they tell about things that man would not discover for millennia to come. For example, God also proved His existence very dramatically by stating medical and scientific truths long before any human could have possibly known about them. The examples of these startling statements could easily fill several books, but I thought it might be interesting to bring up just a few of them here.

Let's look first in the area of medicine. One of my favorites is found in Genesis 17:12, when God said, *"For the generations to come every male among you who is eight days old must be circumcised."*

The eight days mentioned is the interesting part. Only recently in modern medicine have doctors found that when a baby is born, they have no bacteria in their intestines for the first few days. By the seventh day, the bacteria multiply and produce vitamin K. Without vitamin K and prothrombin protein (which is produced by the liver using vitamin K), the blood will not clot properly and the possibility of severe bleeding as well as infection would make circumcision very dangerous in the early Jewish communities. It is quite obvious that only God would have known such a thing back then.

Actually, God gave the Israelites a lot of instruction over three thousand years ago that no one at that time could have possibly known the reason for. For instance, the existence of germs was not discovered until 1890; however, God obviously knew about them and gave the Jews a whole lot of instruction about hygiene and sanitation. I could literally list dozens of

verses on those subjects, but as a way of example we can read
God's instruction in Leviticus 6:28 about cooking meat in a pot, *"the pot is to be scoured and rinsed with water."* God had these words written down before 1450 BC.

It is hard for us to believe, but it was only in the mid 1800's that any doctors at all thought that any diseases could be transmitted by anything that we could not see. One of the first was a Hungarian doctor by the name of Ignaz Semmelweis. He noticed that young mothers who gave birth in hospitals were more likely to die than the ones who gave birth in their homes. In fact, the staggering death rate among new hospital birth mothers was between fifteen and thirty percent in 1845 in the hospital where Dr. Semmelweis was practicing. Extremely observant, he noticed that the young interns would examine dead bodies in the morning and immediately go and examine expectant mothers in another ward, without washing their hands. This was the normal practice up to the late 1800's because the concept of germs was unknown.

Dr. Semmelweis began insisting that the interns under him wash vigorously before touching expectant mothers. The mortality rate dropped almost overnight down to two percent.

The striking thing is that the medical staff continued to think his ideas were ridiculous and they fired him. He went to another hospital and instituted the same hand washing procedures with the same results, dropping that hospital's mortality rate from fifteen percent to less than one percent. It still took decades, though, to convince the medical community to change their habits, and even when they did they normally washed in a bowl, where the germs could stay, rather than washing in running water.

This all happened very recently by historical calendars, but God was giving the Israelites instruction to wash with running water thirty five hundred years ago. There are quite a few verses that talk about this, but to take just one example, we can look at Leviticus 15:13,

"And when he who has a discharge is cleansed of his discharge, then he shall count for himself seven days for his cleansing, wash his clothes, and bathe his body in running water; then he shall be clean."

It actually took one of God's medical instructions to stop the terrible black plague that devastated a third of the European population, including some entire villages. No one had ever heard of the notion of quarantine. Doctors gave advice such as to stop eating pepper or garlic. Many thought the problem was caused by the position of the planets. The nightmare was a total mystery to everyone.

Finally, after what seemed like an endless hell on earth, some ministers in Vienna started pouring over the scriptures. The answer was found in Leviticus 13:46, in which God introduced the idea of quarantine. In talking about people who had leprosy or plague like symptoms, God said, *"He shall be unclean. All the days he has the sore he shall be unclean. He is unclean, and he shall dwell alone; his habitation shall be outside the camp."*

The dreaded black plague was finally stopped with the instruction given by God. There is even a statue in the center of Vienna dedicated to the countless black plague victims, and to the church leaders who found the way to end the nightmare in the instructions of the all-knowing God.

Medical science is not God's only strong suit. His words have foretold truth in all areas of science. In astronomy, for example, God asked Job in chapter 38, verse 31, *"Can you bind the beautiful Pleiades?"* Only recently have scientists come to realize that the stars that make up Pleiades are the gravitational center of the Milky Way.

In the next verse Job is asked, *"Can you guide Arcturus?"* We now know that Arcturus is the fastest star in the heavens, traveling at a phenomenal 125,000 miles per second. Can you imagine trying to guide that? Arcturus has, in fact, become known as the "Runaway Star." God obviously knows everything.

Statements like these that God made are scattered throughout the entire Bible. People sometimes say, though, that God did not go into enough detail about such things as the creation for modern man to believe in it. Now, let's be serious, can you imagine if God had tried to explain cosmic proper time, E=MC2, gravitational pull, time dilation, and the like, to the readers of His Word prior to today. None of it would have made any sense to them at all.

We need to realize that although everything God said was fact, His Bible is not meant to be a complete encyclopedia of every-thing He knows. If it were, there would not be room enough for it on planet earth, and no mortal could ever read it in a lifetime. That was not the purpose of His Word. The purpose was to prove to us that He exists, and to lay out His plan for you and I to be able to spend eternity with Him. Interspersed in that, we also find out some of the characteristics of who He is.

That being said, though, it is awesomely amazing to see how God proves His existence with ultra-simple phrases that eventually become meaningful as mankind learns a smattering more about the marvelous universe He created. Some of those little phrases are complete mysteries to the human finite brain for hundreds and thousands of years.

One such phrase that mystified me is found in Hebrews 1:10-12, which says, *"In the beginning, O Lord, you laid the foundations of the earth, and the heavens are the work of your hands. They will perish, but you remain; they will all wear out like a garment. You will roll them up like a robe; like a garment they will be changed. But You remain the same, and your years will never end."*

What struck me so odd was the phrase, *"You will roll them up like a robe."* It just didn't make sense to me at all. I knew there was universe in every direction from the earth. To me the entire universe must be like a ball. How in the world could God roll up the universe like a garment if it was a ball? It would have to be flat to do that. Can you see the problem I struggled with?

Now comes the hottest thing in science, string theory. It is only about twenty years old and every new physicist and mathematician wants to specialize in it. Many string theory scientists believe it holds the answers to everything in the universe. It is the basis for all the popular Matrix movies, so it must be important stuff.

The basic thought of string theory is that everything taken to its base form is made up of energy that is in the shape of a string. The latest discovery in string theory physics is that these "strings" make up membranes, cleverly called "branes". These branes can be infinitesimally small, or they can be gigantic. The newest suggestion coming out of "brane" physics is that all of the universe exists on one "brane", a relatively flat surface, kind of like a piece of cloth, or would you believe, a "robe." If this theory is true, and scientists all seem to agree that it is, then God could truly roll the universe up "like a robe." Some of the simplest statements in God's Word are turning out to be the most awesome.

As a total aside, string theory also says that our universe, our spacial dimension, is like a slice of bread in a loaf. It claims that there are parallel universes, the other slices in the loaf. We may not know that this is indeed true until we cross the line we call death, but it may be that heaven is a parallel dimension to what we currently live on. Many verses in the Bible allude to something like that.

String theory even talks about something it calls "worm holes", which are actually tunnel like holes that exist between the parallel dimensions. In other words, these are tunnel like openings between the universes in which something could travel back and forth between the two. Does that sound to you like the tunnels constantly described by people who have had near death experiences. It does to me. It also sounds a lot like descriptions of things mentioned in the Bible, such as Jacob's ladder. This has nothing to do with the purpose of this book, but I personally believe it all makes sense, and I also believe that there could well be the main "worm hole" over Jerusalem. If so, that would explain so much that is in the Bible.

I think this entire concept can become food for a lot of pondering for all of us. For now, though, let's return to things that God told us in advance that are totally provable, things that leave no doubt about His existence, and more.

Chapter Eight

The one question that has haunted mankind forever, the existence of God, can be put to rest when we do it His way. We need only pay heed to His own words, *"I am God, and there is none like me. I make known the end from the beginning, from ancient times, what is still to come."* Isaiah 46:10. Then, when we realize that the one and only place in the world where we can find an infallible list of fulfilled prophecies that could only have been made from outside our time and space is the Bible, we can know for a certainty that not only does God exist, but that He communicated to us through that Bible.

After approximately fifteen thousand hours of research into the Bible, I can attest to the fact that only someone outside of our dimension could have written it. I know that sounds like an incredible statement to make, but I find it to be even more true with every additional hour I spend in studying it. Very few people, of course, have even actually read it, so the information most people get about the Bible comes from other people, most of whom themselves have not read it, including the skeptics I have encountered. Plus, I can tell you that even reading it through five times does not prepare a person for the complexity of it when deep research is actually undertaken.

No other book even comes close to the genius of the Bible. We are barely scratching the surface of that genius in this book. Professor Harold Gans, a noted mathematician with over 180 technical papers to his credit, and a senior U.S. Army codes consultant, started studying the Bible as a complete skeptic. After several years he concluded that the Bible had to have been written by God, and He had to have written it in a single second. The intricate weaving of an unknown myriad of things throughout the entire 66 books of the Bible, both on the surface, and underlying it, according to Gans, "is far beyond human scope, even with the help of the most sophisticated computers."

If that is the case, and I truly believe it is, does that mean that the other question that plagues mankind can be answered with research into this communication from outside our realm? The question I naturally am referring to is whether or not it makes any difference at all which religion a person subscribes to, or are all religions the same. If, as God's Word tells us, *"It is to the glory of God to conceal a matter; to search out a matter is the glory of kings."* Proverbs 25:2, let's search out the matter.

The deeper we search the more we find that there actually are many ways that God used to predict the future or explain things. One of the more fascinating to me is with His use of names throughout His Word. To start with we need to be aware that Hebrew names all had a meaning, kind of like the native American Indian names. For example, let's look at ten biblical names and their meanings:

1 - Adam means "man"
2 - Enoch means "teaching"
3 - Enosh means "mortal"
4 - Jared means "shall come down"
5 - Kenan means "sorrow"
6 - Lamech means "despairing"
7 - Mahalalel means "blessed God"
8 - Methuselah means "his death shall bring"
9 - Noah means "comfort"
10 - Seth means "is appointed"

These ten names were not taken at random. They actually comprise the first genealogy given in the Bible in Genesis 5. We listed those names in alphabetical order, but in Genesis they are obviously listed in chronological order; Adam, Seth, Enosh, Kenan, Mahalalel, Jared, Enoch, Methuselah, Lamech, and finally Noah.

I hope you are sitting down for this, for when we read the meanings of those names a sentence is formed, which reads: "Man is appointed mortal sorrow, (but) blessed God shall come down, teaching (that) His death shall bring the despairing comfort."

In the very first book in the Bible God spelled out what was going to happen. Mankind was, in fact, appointed mortal sorrow, since God had said that if man ate of the tree of the knowledge of good and evil, he would surely die. That is truly mortal sorrow. But that hidden prophecy tells us that God Himself would come to earth, teaching that His death would bring life. What a phenomenal prophecy, and it was couched in a simple genealogy.

We can imagine that since God proved His existence with fulfilled prophecy, He probably would want to prove with prophecies who He would be when He appeared in human form. And as we will see, He did exactly that in such a convincing manner that no one who looks at the evidence could possible deny it.

When we consider prophecies, we need to repeat the fact that of the thousands of "holy books" of the thousands of religions that exist on earth, not one of them contains a single fulfilled prophecy, with the glaring exception of the Bible. That in itself is a startling statement, and even more so since we know that every one of the thousands of Biblical predictions that were supposed to have happened by now have indeed taken place, often very dramatically.

Without knowing the facts, some would think that what I just wrote about other holy books could not possibly be true, but it is. Recently an e-mail circulated so continuously in cyberspace that I would estimate that I received it myself no less than a dozen times. You may have, too. At the end of that e-mail, which listed a lot of interesting facts about Iraq, was a purported quote from the Koran which talked about the events of 9/11 and issued a warning to the planners. This quote was a complete hoax. There is no such verse in the Koran. And, as is true with all other "holy books," absolutely none of the very few prophecies found in that Islamic book have ever been fulfilled.

It bears repeating, there has never been a single fulfilled prophecy in any "holy book" of the thousands that exist, other than the Bible. And every prophecy in the Bible that should have been fulfilled by now has indeed come true. Additionally the number of such fulfilled foretellings in the Bible is staggering, numbering into the several thousands.

Not only do these fulfilled prophecies prove conclusively that God exists, but they also prove that the Bible was in fact written by God. Should that be at all surprising? Obviously God, who created everything, is more than intelligent enough to be able to communicate with His creation. It is only natural that He would. Hopefully that is becoming as obvious as the fact of God's existence. If not, read on and it will.

Let's go back to the time that we talked about so much in the first part of this book, the period of time in which the Jews were held captive in Babylonia. In the book of Daniel, which was written during that captivity, we read, *"Know and understand this: From the issuing of the decree to restore and rebuild Jerusalem until the Anointed One, the ruler, comes, there will be seven sevens, and sixty two sevens."* Daniel 9:25.

This is one of the most important prophecies that God ever made. It is worth our total attention. And it does not disappoint.

We need to first of all understand that the Hebrew word for "sevens" in this scripture was "shabuwa", which was an idiom like our words decade and score. We all understand that decade means ten years and score means twenty years. In the same way Shabuwa meant seven years. Therefore, this prophecy is saying that sixty nine seven year periods (seven shabuwa and sixty two shabuwa) will pass between the decree to rebuild Jerusalem and the coming of the Anointed One.

If we now do the math we find that 69 times 7 years is 483 years. The years referred to in this case were obviously Jewish years which each contained 360 days. Therefore, 483 times 360 days equals 173,880 days. This number of days will become very important to us so please make a mental note.

Since we now know our history from previous chapters, it is interesting to note that this prophecy was made two years before Cyrus and his Medo/Persian army took over Babylon. As we learned earlier, the Jews were then treated much nicer, and many were allowed to return to their homeland. Jerusalem, however, remained in ruins.

Next we need to look at another character who enters the scene about eighty five years after the date of the prophecy. His name was Nehemiah.

Although, as we have seen, about 42,000 of the Israelites returned to their homeland after Cyrus demolished the Assyrian Empire that had kept them captive for seventy years, most of the Jewish people remained in Babylon where they felt at home, or headed north for better opportunities. One of those who did not go to his ancestors' home of Jerusalem was Nehemiah. He worked his way up to holding the important job as the cup bearer to the king of Persia, Artaxerxes. Obviously Nehemiah was well liked by Artaxerxes to hold such an intimate job.

At this point we will need to know about an event that happened that became pivotal in one of the most important prophecies that exists. We will read Nehemiah's own account.

"*In the month of Kislev in the twentieth year, while I was in the citadel of Susa, Hanani, one of my brothers, came from Judah with some other men, and I questioned them about the Jewish remnant that survived the exile, and also about Jerusalem.*

They said to me, 'Those who survived the exile and are back in the province are in great trouble and disgrace. The wall of Jerusalem is broken down, and its gates have been burned with fire.'

When I heard these things, I sat down and wept. For some days I mourned and fasted and prayed before the God of heaven."Nehemiah 1:1-4.

He continues in chapter 2, "*In the month of Nisan in the twentieth year of King Artaxerxes, when wine was brought for him, I took the wine and gave it to the king. I had not been sad in his presence before; so the king asked me, 'Why does your face look so sad when you are not ill? This can be nothing but sadness of heart.'*

I was very much afraid, but I said to the king, 'May the king live forever! Why should my face not look sad when the city where my fathers are buried lies in ruins, and its gates have been destroyed by fire.'

Then the king said to me, 'What is it you want?'

Then I prayed to the God of heaven, and I answered the king, 'If it pleases the king and your servant has found favor in his sight, let him send me to the city in Judah where my fathers are buried so that I can rebuild it." Nehemiah 2:1-5.

Artaxerxes agrees to the request and writes a decree to that effect, including letters to different governors to give Nehemiah safe passage, and even provide the lumber needed for the rebuilding. Secular history tells us that this decree was made on March 14, 445 BC.

Let's refresh our memory and look once again at the phenomenal prophecy in Daniel 9:25, *"Know and understand this: From the issuing of the decree to restore and rebuild Jerusalem until the Anointed One, the ruler, comes, there will be seven sevens, and sixty two sevens."*

We also learned that to see what was fulfilled we must count forward 173,880 days on the Jewish calendar. When we do, we end up at April 6, 32 AD, which we know was the fourth Feast of Passover in Jerusalem under the reign of Tiberius. Now, hold on to your hat. We also know that April 6, 32 AD was the exact day that Jesus rode into Jerusalem on a donkey and let the crowds praise Him as King.

God foretold over 500 years in advance, to the exact day, the day that His *"Anointed One"* would come.

Let's pause and let this sink in. If we only had one prophecy to look at, this one by itself would prove not only that God exists, but that He communicates to us through the Bible, and additionally that Jesus is the Anointed One.

Furthermore, on that specific date Jesus rode in on a donkey, fulfilling another prophecy in Zechariah 9:9. *"Rejoice greatly, O Daughter of Zion! Shout, Daughter of Jerusalem! See, your king comes to you, righteous and having salvation, gentile and riding on a donkey, on a colt, the foal of a donkey."*

On top of that, the Pharisees knew that predicted date, for they said in Luke 19:39, *"Teacher, rebuke your disciples."* To this Jesus replied in the next verse, *"I tell you, if they keep quiet the stones will cry out."* a reference to a prediction in Joshua 24:27, *"This stone will be a witness against us. It has heard all the words the Lord has said to us. It will be a witness against you if you are untrue to your God."*

The fact is that Jesus had hoped that all the people would have studied the Word of God enough to know the exact day that was foretold in Daniel 9:25. Unfortunately the people had not studied. They had not "searched out the matter," which we learned early on from Proverbs 25, *"is the glory of kings."*

And since they did not know, the scripture tells us just one verse later in Luke 19:41, *"As He approached Jerusalem and saw the city, He wept over it and said, 'If you, even you, had only known on this day what would bring you peace - but now it is hidden from your eyes."* He went on to declare a prophecy, *"The days will come upon you when your enemies will build an embankment against you and encircle you and hem you in on every side. They will dash you to the ground, you and the children within your walls. They will not leave one stone on another, because you did not recognize the time of God's coming to you."*

That prophecy was fulfilled in detail in 70 AD when the Romans destroyed the city and even tore the temple apart stone by stone to get the gold that had melted down the walls when the temple was accidentally torched.

Chapter Nine

The coming of Jesus as the Messiah is the second most prophesied event in God's Word. In fact, the primary purpose of the Old Testament was to alert the people that He was coming, plus to explain the purpose of His earthly visit. There are over three hundred separate prophecies pertaining to Jesus that were all fulfilled in His life. Let's now take a look at just a few of those prophecies in the Old Testament that dealt with the coming of the "Anointed one". We'll start at His earthly beginning.

In Micah 5:2 we read, *"But you, Bethlehem Ephrathah, though you are small among the clans of Judah, out of you will come for me one who will be ruler over Israel, whose origins are from old, from ancient times."*

As every five year old child in our culture knows from Christmas stories, Jesus was born in Bethlehem. The familiar story in Matthew 2:1 relates, *"After Jesus was born in Bethlehem in Judea, during the time of King Herod, Magi from the east came to Jerusalem and asked, 'Where is the* one who has been born king of the Jews? We saw his star in the east and have come to worship Him."

God foresaw that King Herod, when he heard from the Magi that a king had been born, would decide to kill all the baby boys in Bethlehem that were two or under. Since God knew this would happen, He prophesied that He would help Jesus's parents get him to Egypt as a means of escape.

In Hosea 11:1 we read, *"When Israel was a child, I loved him, and out of Egypt I called my son."*

In talking about the slaughter of the baby male children by King Herod, God had foretold in the Old Testament in Jeremiah 15, *"A voice is heard in Ramah, mourning and weeping, Rachel weeping for her children and refusing to be comforted because they are no more."* Four hundred years later we read what actually happened in Matthew 2:16, *"When Herod realized that he had been outwitted by the magi, he was furious, and he gave orders to kill all the boys in Bethlehem and its vicinity who were two years old and under, in accordance with the time he had learned from the Magi."*

Baby Jesus, however was saved as predicted, for in Matthew 2:13, *"An angel of the*

Lord appeared to Joseph in a dream. 'Get up,' he said, 'take the child and his mother and escape to Egypt. Stay there until I tell you, for Herod is going to search for the child to kill Him."

After everything appeared safe, God did indeed call the family back in Matthew 2:19-20, "After Herod died, an angel of the Lord appeared in a dream to Joseph in Egypt and said, 'Get up, take the child and his mother and go to the land of Israel, for those who are trying to take the child's life are dead."

Interestingly, in the next verse we learn, "So he got up, took the child and his mother and went to the land of Israel. But when he heard that Archelaus was reigning in Judea in place of his father, Herod, he was afraid to go there. Having been warned in a dream, he withdrew to the district of Galilee, and he went there to live in a town called Nazareth. So was fulfilled what was said through the prophets: He will be called a Nazarene." Matthew 2:21-22

We might mention at this point that there were several prophecies that foretold the lineage of Jesus. Starting back in Genesis 49:10, written over 1,500 years before Jesus walked the earth, we find the words of the patriarch, Jacob, "The scepter will not depart from Judah, nor the ruler's staff from between his feet, until it comes *to whom it belongs and the obedience of the nations is his."* In both Matthew 1:16 and Luke 3:23 the ancestry of Jesus is traced back to the tribe of Judah. Jesus is even called the Lion of Judah.

Continuing on, we can witness God's foretelling of John the Baptist's preaching preceding Jesus in Isaiah 40:3, *"A voice of one calling: 'In the desert prepare the way for the Lord; make straight in the wilderness a highway for our God."*

Of course, seven hundred years later, John the Baptist, on seeing Jesus, said. *"Look, The Lamb of God, who takes away the sin of the world! This is the one I meant when I said, 'A man who comes after me has surpassed me because he was before me.' I myself did not know him, but the reason I came baptizing in water was that he might be revealed to Israel."* John 1:29-31

I find the rest of that testimony by John the Baptist interesting because Isaiah, writing some seven hundred years earlier had foretold of the Messiah, *"The spirit of the Lord will rest on him."* Isaiah 11:2.

And in John 1:32, John the Baptists continues, *"Then John gave this testimony: 'I saw the Spirit come down from heaven as a dove and remain on Him. I would not have known him, except that the one who sent me to baptize with* water told me, 'The man on whom you see the Spirit come down and remain is He who will baptize with the Holy Spirit.' I have seen and I testify that this is the Son of God."

I must admit that after typing John's closing sentence I had to pause. I was thinking, "what more could be said to add to, '*I have seen and I testify that this is the Son of God.*"

But we will continue on and get into even much more detailed prophetic statements than we have up to now. The way Jesus began His ministry was quite telling, in that His first act of public speaking was to read the scroll of Isaiah 61 in the temple. It, in itself was a foretelling of the ministry of Jesus, and He read, "*The Spirit of the Sovereign Lord is on me, because the Lord has anointed me to preach good news to the poor. He has sent me to bind up the brokenhearted, to proclaim freedom for the captives, and release from darkness the prisoners,*"

Seven hundred years in advance God prophesied first about John the Baptist and then about the well-known event of Jesus driving the money changers out of the temple. In Malachi 3:1-4 we read, "*I will send my messenger, who will prepare the way before me. Then suddenly the Lord you are seeking will come to his temple; the messenger of the covenant, whom you desire, will come,' says the Lord Almighty. 'But who can endure the day of his coming? Who can stand when he appears? For he will be like a refiner's fire or a launderer's soap. He will sit as a refiner and purifier of silver; he will purify the Levites and refine them like gold and silver. Then the Lord will have men who will bring offerings in righteousness."*

The temple, of course, was run by the Levites, as they were the only tribe of Israel who could be priests. In Matthew 21:12 the actual story is told, *"Jesus entered the temple area and drove out all who were buying and selling there; He overturned the tables of the money changers and the benches of those selling doves. 'It is written' He said to them, 'My house will be called a house of prayer, but you are making it a den of robbers."* Jesus cleansed the temple like *"launderer's soap."*

The Levites should have known because in Jeremiah 7:11 God said, about 585 BC, *"Has this house, which bears my Name, become a den of robbers to you? But I have been watching! Declares the Lord."* The prophecies predicted the disciple Judas's roll in history in Psalm 41:9, *"Even my close friend, whom I trusted, he who shared my bread, has lifted up his heel against me."* And God got even more specific over 400 years in advance of his betrayal in Zechariah 11:12, *"I told them, 'If you think it best, give me my pay; but if not, keep it.' So they paid me thirty pieces of silver."*

Of course, the actual event was recorded in the New Testament in Matthew 26:14-15, *"Then one of the twelve - the one called Judas Escariot - went to the chief priests and asked, 'What are you willing to give me if I hand Him over to you?' So they counted out for him thirty pieces of silver."*

We might have thought that Judas, being a disciple, would have known that he wasn't going to get to keep the silver pieces, though, because God foretold exactly what would happen to the blood money in the next verse of Zechariah. Evidently Judas was too busy embezzling as the keeper of the purse to take the time to, *"search out a matter."*

The actual prophecy stated, *"And the Lord said to me, 'Throw it to the potter' - the handsome price at which they priced me! So I took the thirty pieces of silver and threw them into the house of the Lord to the potter."*

The actual event played out in Matthew 26:3-7,

"When Judas, who had betrayed Him, saw that Jesus was condemned, he was seized with

remorse and returned the thirty silver coins to the chief priests and the elders. 'I have sinned,' he said, 'for I have betrayed innocent blood.'

'What is that to us', they replied. 'That's your responsibility.'

So Judas threw the money into the temple and left. Then he went away and hanged himself.

The chief priests picked up the coins and said, 'It is against the law to put this into the treasury, since it is blood money.' so they decided to use the money to buy the potter's field, as a burial place for foreigners."

God had even mentioned "*potter.*"

A few years back *Science Speaks* published an article in which that revered secular publication looked at the probability of one person's life fulfilling eight of the prophecies that the life of Jesus fulfilled. The article was carefully reviewed by an independent committee of the American Scientific affiliation, and then by the Executive Council of the same organization.

Their findings stated, "The study has been found to be dependable and sound in regard to scientific material. The mathematical analysis included is based upon principles of possibility which are thoroughly sound."

The finding they reviewed and found to be true was that the chances of any one man's life fulfilling just eight of the over 300 prophecies is one in ten to the seventeen power. Written out numerically that is: 1 in 100,000,000,000,000,000.

That would be one in a hundred zillion. We have already explored fourteen fulfilled prophecies in the life of Jesus, and we are just beginning. We obviously are way past one in a hundred zillion already.

Chapter Ten

One would think that if the day Jesus was crucified was as monumental as His followers say, God would have put a lot of emphasis on that day in prophecy. As we will learn, He did.

In fact, the very next verse in Daniel after the foretelling of the exact day that Jesus would ride into Jerusalem, by use of the seven sevens and sixty two sevens, we read, *"After the sixty two sevens the Anointed One will be cut off."* Cut off is obviously a reference to His being killed. And throughout the entire Old Testament there is verse after prophetic verse about the very smallest detail of that day of all days.

The first thing that happened to Jesus after Judas betrayed Him was a sham of a trial before the high priest, Caiaphus. Over 700 years earlier God had foretold what would happen next. *"He was oppressed and afflicted, yet he did not open his mouth; he was led like a lamb to the slaughter, and as a sheep before her shearers is silent, so he did not open his mouth."* Isaiah 53:7.

As we might expect from the above prophecy, that is exactly what happened. *Then the high priest stood up and said to Jesus, 'Are you* not going to answer? What is this testimony that these men are bringing against you?' But Jesus remained silent." Matthew 26:62.

In fact, after the sham of the mock trial with Caiaphus, Jesus was taken to Pilate and the same foretold results occurred. *"When He was accused by the chief priests and the elders, He gave no answer. Then Pilate asked Him, 'Don't you hear the testimony they are bringing against you?' But Jesus made no reply, not even to a single charge - to the great amazement of the Governor,"*

Matthew 27:12.

Once again we can look back 700 hundred years earlier and read, *"I offered my back to those who beat me, my cheeks to those who pulled out my beard; I did not hide my face from mocking and spitting."* Isaiah 50:6.

Additionally, in Micah 5:1 we find, *"They will strike Israel's ruler on the cheek with a rod."*

Of course, after the ridiculous trial, Matthew 26:67 says, *"Then they spit in His face and struck Him with their fists. Others slapped him and said, 'Prophesy to us, Christ. Who hit you?"*

We all know that, *"Two robbers were crucified with him, one on His right and one on his left."* Matthew 27:38, but we should realize that God foretold that fact also, *"he poured out his life* unto *death, and was numbered with the transgressors."* Isaiah 53:12.

The painful spikes driven in His hands and feet were explained hundreds of years earlier in places like Zechariah 12:10, *"they will look on me, the One they have pierced,"* and Isaiah 53:5, *"But he was pierced for our transgressions."* Even the vinegar was foretold that we read about in Luke 23:36, which says, *"The soldiers also came up and mocked Him. They offered him wine vinegar."* We know from Psalm 69:21, written centuries before, *"They put gall in my food and gave me vinegar for my thirst."* The "gall" part even came true for we read, *"There they offered Jesus wine to drink, mixed with gall."*

Matthew 27:34.

Dozens and dozens of very detailed accounts of that day were told in prophetic verses hundreds of years in advance. God, the Father, did want us to pay attention to that day, even down to the part that is spoken of in Psalm 22:18, *"They divide my garments among them and cast lots for my clothing."*

That prophecy was indeed fulfilled. *"When the soldiers crucified Jesus, they took His clothes, divided them into four shares, one for each of them, with the undergarment remaining. This garment was seamless, woven in one piece from top*

91

to bottom. *'Let's not tear it,' they said to one another. 'Let's decide by lot who will get it."*

John 19:23-24.

As an aside, Roman crucifixion, which had not even been invented until about 500 years after most of the many prophecies were given that described the death of Jesus in so much detail, could take several days to result in death. It was a slow, agonizing death.

There were times, however, that the Roman soldiers needed to speed up the death. This was the case with Jesus, since they wanted it all to be finished prior to the next day's Jewish Sabbath. In order to speed up the process the soldiers normally broke the legs of the victims with a club, since the only way to breathe on a cross was to push the body up with the legs. In the prophetic Psalm 34:20, God relates in advance about Jesus, *"He protects all his bones, not one of them will be broken."*

The disciple John, who was there throughout the entire ordeal reports to us, *"But when they came to Jesus they found that He was already dead, they did not break His legs."*

Through Isaiah, God showed what would happen when the crucifixion was over, *"He was assigned a grave with the wicked, and with the rich in his death, though he had done no violence, nor was any deceit in his mouth."* Isaiah 53:9.

This prophecy, too, was fulfilled. *"As evening approached, there came a rich man from Arimathea, named Joseph, who had himself become a disciple of Jesus. Going to Pilate, he asked for Jesus' body, and Pilate ordered that it be given to him. Joseph took the body, wrapped it in clean linen cloth, and placed it in his own new tomb that he had cut out of a rock. He rolled a big rock in front of the entrance and went away."* Matthew 27:57-60.

In this chapter we looked at eleven more of the prophecies about that infamous day in history, and there are others. For the moment, though, let's stop and consider once and for all the probabilities of one man fulfilling the twenty five that we have mentioned so far. In the last chapter we learned that the chances were one in a hundred zillion that one man could have fulfilled just eight of the fourteen we had covered. Can you wrap your mind around the number that would come up for the chance of any one man fulfilling twenty five of these prophecies?

Dr. Grant Jeffrey, in his book, The Signature of God, which I wholeheartedly recommend, did come up with the answer for the chance of one man's life fulfilling seventeen of such prophecies. The startling figure is one in 480,000,000,000,000,000,000,000,000,000,000,000.

That is one in 480 billion, times a billion, times a trillion. And that is only seventeen prophecies. We have studied twenty five.

Jesus fulfilled over three hundred. There never was a debate, if mankind had only looked at what was right in front of them.

As we have already discussed, God is outside our time and space constraints. The Word of God, like Him, was written outside our time and space constraints as well. It was given to normal men to write, but the words came from outside our time.

Second Timothy 3:16 says, *"All scripture is God breathed."*

I mention this, before we leave this chapter dealing with the day of the crucifixion of Jesus, because I think you will find it sobering to read a Psalm, written many centuries earlier, that was so obviously written by Jesus Himself describing that day. Hebrews 2:11-12 even tells us that these are the words of Jesus. I am convinced you will never read the 22nd Psalm the same way again. You will be stunned as you actually discover what was going through the mind of the man, Jesus, as He hung on the cross for those excruciating hours on that day of all days.

"My God, my God, why have you forsaken me? Why are you so far from saving me, so far from the words of my groaning? O my God, I cry out by day, but you do not answer, by night, and am not silent. Yet you are enthroned as the Holy One.

I am poured out like water, and all my bones are out of joint. My heart has turned to wax; it has melted away within me. My strength is dried up like a potsherd, and my tongue sticks to the roof of my mouth; you lay me in the dust of death.

Dogs have surrounded me; a band of evil men has encircled me, they have pierced my hands and feet. I can count all my bones; people stare and gloat over me.

They divide my garments among them and cast lots for my clothing.

But you, O Lord, be not far off, O my Strength, come quickly to help me. Deliver my life from the sword, my precious life from the power of the dogs.

I will declare your name to my brothers; in the congregation I will praise you.

You who fear the Lord, praise him! All you descendants of Jacob, honor him! Revere him, all you descendants of Israel! For he has not despised or disdained the suffering of the afflicted one, he has not hidden his face from him but has listened to his cry for help.

From you comes the theme of my praise in the great assembly; before those who fear you will I fulfill my vows.

The poor will eat and be satisfied; they who seek the Lord will praise him - may your hearts live forever!

All the ends of the earth will remember and turn to the Lord, and all the families of the nations will bow down before him, for dominion belongs to the Lord and he rules over the nations.

Chapter Eleven

You and I may not know each other at all. If we do have a passing acquaintance, we probably don't know each other very well. That is natural. Even people who have been around each other for some time don't truly know each other's real goals, desires, likes and dislikes, challenges and fears. Once we start developing a relationship, be it friendship or love, the way we open up is by sharing our memories.

Jesus was human. Even the staunchest debater doesn't question that. We know for certain that He lived, so He was human. Even Flavius Josephus, the well-respected Jewish historian mentioned Jesus twice in his historic works, and Josephus was definitely not a believer that Jesus was the Messiah.

Josephus was born in 37 AD, a few years after Jesus was crucified, lived until 100 AD, and probably knew some of the same people Jesus knew. But Josephus was a Jew. He had even been a priest before he became commander of the Jewish forces in Galilee until 70 AD when Rome destroyed Jerusalem. He spent his latter years in Rome under the patronage of Roman Emperors who commissioned him to write the History of the Hebrew people. He remained a staunch believer in Judaism.

The Greek translations of the works of Josephus probably have been tampered with by followers of Jesus because they do read as if he, too, may have been a follower, but we can be certain that, in truth, he never abandoned his Jewish heritage.

We can, however, look at the ancient Arabic version of what Josephus wrote of the period, and be confident that it is accurate. In that version we read, "Similarly Josephus the Hebrew (sic). For he says in the treatises that he has written on the governance of the Jews: 'At this time there was a wise man who was called Jesus. And his conduct was good, and he was known to be virtuous. And many people from among the Jews and the other nations became his disciples. Pilate condemned him to be crucified and to die."

Later in the written history of Josephus, the Greek and Arabic translations agree exactly that his original writings included the following paragraph concerning the martyrdom of the half-brother and leader of the first Christian church in Jerusalem, "Since Ananus was that kind of person, and because he perceived an opportunity with Festus having died and Albinus not yet arrived, he called a meeting of the Sanhedrin and brought James, the brother of Jesus (who is called 'Messiah') along with some others. He accused them of transgressing the law, and handed them over for stoning."

It is interesting to historians that James was referred to as the "brother of Jesus" when it was always common in the writings of Josephus to refer to someone as "the son of" someone. Nowhere else does Josephus, in all of his voluminous work, delineate someone as someone else's brother. Evidently Josephus did at least recognize that Jesus was someone very special. At any rate, there is not any question that Jesus lived, or for that matter, that He was crucified.

So, we have this man, a regular human, who has gathered some other regular guys around Him and they are starting to become friends. They obviously liked each other or they would not have stayed together beyond the first few days. And in the evenings after supper they naturally sat around the fire for a while in the evenings and talked. There is nothing at all strange about that. Had we lived back then, you and I could imagine fitting in, kind of like being at camp, or college, or some other situation in which we are getting to know the people we are fairly newly associated with.

The natural progression of opening up to each other would have occurred, and gradually the people would have shared memories; memories of their home lives, memories of the towns they grew up in, memories of events from their past. This is how we let people know about us. This give and take of memories inevitably became more personal. It always does. Then Jesus shared this memory, *"I saw Satan fall like lightning from heaven."* Luke 10:18.

Can you imagine the quietness that ensued? "What did He just say?" Thoughts have got to be running all over the place, like, "I've never known Jesus to lie to us, but He now is saying that He was in heaven When Satan fell, and he saw the whole thing." The Bible doesn't give us the reaction of those present that evening, but we can surely imagine at least the diversity of thoughts at that moment in that little band of "regular guys."

And that was not the only very odd thing that he shared with them as they became closer to each other. He often matter of factly made references to actually having been in heaven, and having seen things that "regular guys" just don't see. At one point He said, *"Your father Abraham rejoiced at the thought of seeing my day, he saw it and was glad.*

'You are not yet fifty years old', the Jews said to Him, 'and you have seen Abraham!'

'I tell you the truth,' Jesus answered, 'before Abraham was born, I am."   John 8:56-58.

Not only did He tell them that He witnessed it, but He said the unthinkable by calling Himself, "I am"; the same name that God told Moses to tell the Israelites when asked who had sent him, *"God said to Moses, 'I AM WHO I AM. This is what you are to say to the Israelites: I AM has sent me to you."*   Exodus 3:14.

This obviously is pretty crazy stuff from an ordinary, moral teacher. As we noted, Jesus was either a liar, a lunatic, or both; or else He was God in the flesh.

In Luke 15:7 Jesus said, *"I tell you that in the same way there will be more rejoicing in heaven over one sinner who repents than over ninety-nine righteous persons who do not need to repent."* Now let's be serious, how was He supposed to know stuff like that unless He had been there?

And not only did He constantly talk about having seen things in heaven first hand, but He continually made statements that sounded like He thought the world revolved around Him and that He was somehow perfect. For instance, Jesus blatantly said in Matthew 28:16, *"All authority in heaven and on earth has been given to me."*

This crazy talk of His was constant. He said, *"Do not think that I have come to abolish the law and the prophets; I have not come to abolish them but to fulfill them."*   Matthew 5:17.

He even dared to say, *"I am the way and the truth and the life. No one comes to the Father except through me."*   John 14:6.

Nobody continually says stuff like that without having everyone around him get fed up with such ludicrous remarks and walking away. Wouldn't you if someone you knew kept on making such grandiose statements about himself? Confucius, Mohamed, Gandhi, and Buddha never talked like that. They were smarter than that. They knew that everyone would be so totally turned off that they would end up telling their stories to a wall.

So why did this band of friends stay around Jesus? The answer is simple: at the same time Jesus was talking crazy, he was also performing miracle after miracle after miracle. And these were not little magic tricks. These were things like turning water into wine, healing crippled people, giving sight to the blind, hearing to the deaf, and even raising the dead. Obviously these things were not myths, because the disciples stayed. There is no other logical answer.

Let's face it; Jesus even claimed to be God. That's right, He did. Although debaters have said that Jesus made no claim, their comments come from lack of knowledge. And interestingly, Jesus made the claim over and over, and in different ways.

In the story of the Samaritan woman at the well, we read, *"The woman said, 'I know that Messiah' (called Christ) 'is coming. When he comes he will explain everything to us.' Then Jesus declared, 'I who speak to you am He."* John 4:25-26.

Then in Matthew 16:15-17, *"But what about you?' He asked, 'Who do you say I am?' Simon Peter answered, 'You are the Christ, the Son of the living God.' Jesus replied, 'Blessed are you, Simon son of Jonah, for this was not revealed to you by man, but by my Father in heaven."*

In John 12:45, *"When he looks at Me, he sees the one who sent Me."*

Also, *"If you really knew Me you would know My Father as well. From now on, you do know him and have seen him."* John 14:7.

In Matthew 26:63, *"The high priest said to Him, 'I charge you under oath by the living God: Tell us if you are the Christ, the Son of God.'*
"Yes it is as you say,' Jesus replied."

Those around Him listened to all these outlandish claims, and we can be sure that initially at least, they wondered. But the miracles kept happening, and as may be the case with you or me, the doubts eventually vanished. They knew. They believed.

Then, they saw Jesus die on that cross. It was obvious that He felt pain like any man. He bled like any man. He died like any one of them would have, had they, too, been crucified.

Nothing that He said had really been provable. Not really. The miracles were phenomenal. But in the end, Jesus bled, and Jesus died. Their dream world came crashing down. Jesus was, in the end, human.

This was a confused, scared, embarrassed group of eleven. Judas, one of their own, was dead. Jesus, their leader, their hope for high government appointments when Jesus established his kingdom, was in the tomb. All they wanted to do was hide. How could they have been so dumb as to have wasted three years of their lives following a lunatic? Obviously that was what He had been. He couldn't have even been just a liar, because a liar would not have lied his way to a Roman flogging and a heinous death on a cross. A liar would have stopped short of that. No, He had to have been a complete lunatic. And they had all been duped.

But what about the miracles? They obviously weren't fake. Maybe God had just answered the prayers of a lunatic. Surely they had seen God answer prayers before. That must have been the only logical answer the eleven could think of. A lunatic that somehow got His prayers answered. God, in his mercy, probably answered the prayers for those blind and deaf folks.

You and I hear people today say that Jesus was just a good, moral, wise teacher. We can be sure that the disciples didn't for a minute entertain that option. No, if Jesus was not God, he was just a lunatic, crazy as a bat, and they were the dumbest eleven men on the planet. We can be sure that John, Andrew, Peter, and James couldn't wait to get back to the solitude of their lives as fisherman on that big Lake of Galilee. They probably didn't ever even want to hear the name Jesus again. What a nightmare!

Those eleven had the advantage of living with Jesus for over three years, but you and I have an advantage that they did not have. You and I have seen the precision of God's Word. We have seen how God told man about such things as germs, long before people knew things existed that were smaller than the eye could see. We have seen that Pleiades really is the gravitational center of the Milky Way.

You and I know that God mentioned Arcturus, and it is indeed the "Runaway Star." Those eleven couldn't have imagined that there was anything like String Theory that would prove that God was right when he alluded to rolling up the flat universe like a ball. There are scores of things that we now know, that they didn't have a clue about.

On top of all those things, they didn't have all of the fulfilled prophecy that we have today. They most certainly could not even guess that their nation would be disbanded, but come back together in one incredible day, just as predicted, and that miracle upon miracle, Israel would become a nation on the very date, May 15, 1948, that the Sovereign God said would be the date.

Those eleven had lived with Jesus, but you and I have God's very own Word that has proven over and over and over to be completely supernatural. Without it, we too, might be deceived and destroyed.

No, the disciples did not know for a certainty, like we now do, that God's Word is so utterly infallible. And they could not see the big picture, like we can. If God had given them the knowledge He has given us, they might have been more open to expect what came next. They might have expected a risen Jesus.

Chapter Twelve

It is completely incredible to realize that you and I can know more about Jesus than the disciples did the day after Christ was crucified. But it is true. Ponder it for a moment and you will be totally amazed. Yes, they had been with the Master for three years, and they had seen first-hand not only His love, gentleness, and wisdom, but also His supernatural power.

On the other hand, not only do we have so many more fulfilled prophecies that obviously strengthen our "knowing," but we also have the entire New Testament, which teaches us so much that they could not know about the big picture of why Jesus came and His plans for the future. Granted, books of the New Testament are titled with names of some of those original eleven, like Matthew, John, and Peter, but we must remember that although their names are on those books, it was the Holy Spirit of God who was truly the author. The second book of Timothy, verse 3:16, tells us emphatically, *"All scripture is God breathed."*

People of today too readily forget that fact; *"All scripture is God breathed."* It wasn't men who could see into the future the phenomenal fulfillment of the prophecies we have studied. It was God. We are told, *"For prophecy never had its origin in the will of man, but men spoke from God as they were carried along by the Holy Spirit."*   2 Peter 1:21.

The same is true of every other word in the sixty six books of the Bible. Every single letter was *"God breathed."* Jesus told us in Matthew 5:18, *"I tell you the truth, until heaven and earth disappear, not the smallest letter, not the least stroke of the pen, will by any means disappear from the Law until everything is accomplished."* Actually, this is one scripture that I prefer the King James Version which says, *"For verily I say unto you, till heaven and earth pass, one jot or one tittle shall in no wise pass from the law, till all be fulfilled."*

There is just something about the archaic words *"one jot or one tittle"* that creates more of a mental picture for me than *"stroke of the pen."* In either case, though, the meaning is clear; every single letter in the Bible was authored by God. Everything is there for a reason. Every single phrase has a meaning. And remember,

"It is the glory of God to conceal a matter; to search out a matter is the glory of kings." Proverbs 25:2.

The eleven disciples did have the thirty nine books of the Old Testament, but not one of the twenty seven books of the New Testament had been dictated by the Father until some years after Jesus was crucified, and there are things revealed in each of those books that probably were unknown by the disciples the day He died. Obviously they knew nothing about the resurrection and its meaning for mankind, because it had not even occurred, but also they knew nothing about the future events of the world, like we can know by studying the books of the New Testament. As we said, it is a truly awesome thought that we can know more about God and His plan just by sitting in our living room and reading our Bible than the men knew who actually walked with Jesus every day of his three year ministry. To not take advantage of such a privilege may be the most absurd act of modern man.

It's not that our society doesn't read. Every single day virtually everyone in every nation reads something. We read novels. We read magazines. We read business and trade materials. We read meaningless gossip columns. We read inane forwarded e-mail jokes. We read advertisements. We even read comic strips. For goodness sake, we even read cereal boxes as we eat our breakfasts. But we do not as a whole ever read the most important words ever written; words that came directly from the mind of the Creator and Author of everything.

God was loving enough to give us His thoughts and plans; everything we need to know for our lives on this earth and beyond into eternity; yet sadly, less than 50% of the people in North America can even name the first book in God's Word. Just to be clear, it is Genesis.

It isn't that we are living five hundred years ago and don't have access to God's Word. The average American household owns three Bibles, and 92% of the individuals own at least one copy. The Bible is the world's all-time best seller, with twenty million copies sold each year. Gideons International even gives away forty five million copies a year.

Polls tell us, though, that 80% say the Bible is too confusing to read. How many of those do you think ever even opened one up and tried. 64% say they are just too busy to read it. As a result one third of Americans think Billy Graham delivered the Sermon on the Mount. One fourth don't even know why Easter is celebrated. Even a remarkable 80% of people who claim to be "born again Christians" think that the Bible says "God helps those that help themselves," which was really said by Ben Franklin.

God gave us the commandment in several places to read his Word daily. For instance, Joshua 1:8 commands us, *"Do not let this Book of the Law depart from your mouth; meditate on it day and night."*

In fact, listen to how detailed God was in telling us to keep His Word in front of us at all times, *"These commandments that I give you today are to be upon your hearts. Impress them on your children. Talk about them when you sit at home and when you walk along the road, when you lie down and when you get up. Tie them as symbols on your hands and bind them on your foreheads. Write them on the doorframes of your houses and on your gates."* Deuteronomy 6:6-9.

Instead, though, man reads his cereal box. Is it any wonder that the debaters on both sides can give no proofs for their opinions? God hit it on the head when He said in Hosea 4:6, *"My people are destroyed from lack of knowledge."*

There is a cute but profound little statement, "Bible means *B*asic *I*nstruction *B*efore *L*eaving *E*arth." We won't get that on a Wheaties box. Enough said.

Getting back to our point of departure, the eleven disciples on that fateful day Jesus was crucified did not have the knowledge we can have. They knew enough, however, to know that Jesus could not have been only a good, wise, moral teacher. The statements He had made over and over precluded that option, unless He also was God.

Those today who label Jesus as only a good, wise, and moral teacher don't realize that they, too, do not really have the option to call Him that. He was either God or He was a lunatic. The proof of which one he actually was lies in one place, the empty tomb.

Everything having to do with Jesus revolves around that one place. Nothing else matters in discussing Jesus unless we can resolve the question about the resurrection. Anything else is irrelevant until that is proved or disproved. The Bible even makes that fact totally clear for it says, *"And if Christ has not been raised, our preaching is useless and so is your faith. More than that, we are then found to be false witnesses about God, for we have testified about God that he raised Christ from the dead. But he did not raise Him if in fact the dead are not raised. For if the dead are not raised, then Christ has not been raised either. And if Christ has not been raised, your faith is futile; you are still in your sins. Then those also who have fallen asleep in Christ are lost. If only for this life we have hope in Christ, we are to be pitied more than all men."* 1 Corinthians 15:14-19.

You and I, who have seen some of the over six thousand dramatically fulfilled prophecies, know not only that God exists; we also know that the Bible is God's communication with us. And we can also know totally from God's Word that Christ arose from the dead. We can concur with the scores of statements such as that of the Psalmist, *"All your words are true."* Psalms 119:160.

For a doubter, though, who has not come to that solid knowledge, is there any way to prove that not only was there an empty tomb, but that Jesus Christ really and truly arose from the dead after three days, exactly as He said He would? Although God's *"words are true,"* is there any outside historical proof?

The best place to start is to go to the most trusted historian of that day, Flavius Josephus. He was a Jew who would have wanted to disprove everything about Jesus if he could have, but he was first and foremost an honest historian. Let's look at his unbiased historical entry about Jesus, using the extremely reliable Arabic translation:

"At this time there was a wise man who was called Jesus. And His conduct was good, and He was known to be virtuous. And many people from among the Jews and the other nations became His disciples. Pilate condemned Him to be crucified and to die. And those who became his disciples did not abandon His discipleship. They reported that He had appeared to them after His crucifixion and that he was alive; accordingly, He was perhaps the Messiah concerning whom the prophets have recounted wonders."

By Flavius Josephus.

We need to be crystal clear about one very important fact in reading the above report from Josephus in this account that he knew was going to be part of the official history of the Jewish people; Josephus was a Jew's Jew. He did not have a Christian bone in his body. If there had been any way at all to squelch the idea that Jesus rose from the dead, Josephus would have surely included it. Like all religious Jews of his time, he would have mentioned anything he could have in order to stop the spread of Christianity.

It was the Jewish religious community that pushed for the crucifixion of Jesus in the first place. They hated Him and wanted him dead because they considered Him a threat to their way of life and their standing in the community. Josephus knew all of that, and if he could have been some assistance to the Jewish cause, he would gladly have done it. Fortunately, though, Josephus was above all a historian. He wanted his masterpiece Jewish history to be completely true and accurate. Therefore, there is not even a hint in it that there was any proof that the resurrection did not occur. That glaring omission speaks volumes.

Let's be realistic, if there had been a way to stop any talk about a risen Jesus, not only the Jewish leaders, but the Romans as well, would have done it. If they could have produced a body, there is no question but that they would have quickly done it. Obviously, nobody could be produced.

It's not as if Jesus was buried in a secret tomb. Everyone knew where it was to begin with, but in fairness to any skeptics we won't even go into any of the Biblical accounts here. We will look totally at outside facts. The only viable option to the resurrection really happening was that the disciples stole the body and perpetrated a hoax.

Roman soldiers were very skilled at their work of crucifying criminals. Jesus did not come off that cross alive. Pilate himself was involved in this crucifixion. The captain in charge would have been very, very sure that the accused man, Jesus, was dead. We don't even have to read the Biblical accounts of the soldiers sticking a spear in him to be sure of that. We can know from common sense that Jesus died. Not only the Romans, but the Jewish leaders would have made very sure that Jesus, their nemesis, was very, very dead.

So, as we said, since it is irrefutable that everyone but the disciples of Jesus would have wanted it known that Jesus not only died, but that He stayed dead, there are only two plausible options; either He arose, or the disciples stole his body and from then on lied.

Not too many years after the crucifixion, the first letter to the Corinthians was sent by Paul. In it, he made the following statement about Jesus after He supposedly arose, *"He appeared to Peter, and then to the Twelve* (By this time Judas had been replaced with Matthias). *After that he appeared to more than five hundred of the brothers at the same time, most of whom are still living, though some have fallen asleep. Then He appeared to James, then to all the apostles."*

1 Corinthians 5:5-6.

We don't offer this scripture as proof of anything. We only quote it because we know that this letter by Paul was widely circulated. Don't you imagine that if there had been any way to disprove the claim that five hundred people saw a risen Jesus at the same time, the Jewish leaders would have done it. Surely they could have gotten one of that crowd to confess that it was a lie if it was. We have to realize that the Jewish leaders had a lot at stake, and they obviously had a whole lot of power. But again, they could bring no one forward to admit that Paul had lied. We can be sure that Josephus would have put at least one paragraph in his report had they found only one talkative soul.

Let's not lose sight of the fact that, knowing how easy it is to prove God's existence by his fulfilled prophecies, and knowing also how easy it is to prove that he communicated to us through the Bible by not only his prophecies but the other amazing examples we have looked at, and knowing that the life and death of Jesus fulfilled all three hundred of the prophecies of the coming Anointed One, it is ludicrous for us not to just take God's Word for the fact that Jesus arose. However, in case anyone could possibly think they need more, we'll continue to explore the option of what would be the biggest hoax in history.

We can know a little more by looking at the disciples themselves. These were not educated men. They were ordinary laborers. From what they even wrote about themselves we can grasp that they probably were not the sharpest tools in the shed. None of them were public speakers, which even back then, as today, was one of the scariest things for anyone not accustomed to it to do. And they obviously were not the bravest bunch around because we know they all scattered and went into hiding when Jesus was arrested. Sure, Peter was a hot head, but as far as we know only John was even brave enough to witness the crucifixion.

So what did they have to gain by fabricating a story about Jesus rising from the dead? Without that story they could return to their peaceful lives as fisherman and the like. By concocting such a ridiculous story they knew that they would be hunted down, tortured, and probably killed. Obviously a lie like that wasn't going to bring them riches. The truth is that they had nothing at all to gain by such a hoax.

But let's suppose they did in fact make up the whole thing, fearful as they were of the authorities, and even of having to persuade large groups of people by preaching it. The only possible reason could have been to somehow save face for having been so gullible as to have followed a lunatic. Remember, that was their only real choice at the time of describing Jesus. Without a true resurrection these disciples had to believe that Jesus was crazy. They were smart enough to know that no sane man would lie about something that he knew would get him tortured and killed.

Modern man, of course, should be just as smart as those disciples were. No sane man would make up a lie that would gain him nothing, knowing that that lie would bring about his own torture and death. And here lies the biggest proof of all.

These timid disciples set out in different directions, mostly on their own, to tell people this incredible story which would bring them no gain whatsoever, knowing the consequences. Most had little or no contact with each other. Let's see what happened to them.

Simon Peter started out preaching this remarkable tale in Jerusalem before he eventually reached Rome. He was executed by Nero by crucifixion either in 64 or 67 AD, however unlike Jesus, he was head down.

Andrew, Peter's brother, went to Achaia (Southern Greece) and Scythia (Ukraine and Southern Russia). Like his brother and Jesus, Andrew was also crucified, however his crucifixion was spread eagle style, and his death took three excruciating days.

James stayed and preached in what is now modern Israel. He might have traveled farther except he was beheaded by King Herod Agrippa I in 44 AD.

Philip went to Phygia in central Turkey, where he was tied to a pillar and stoned to death.

Bartholomew really got around. He preached in what is now Iraq, Iran, Turkey, India, Egypt, Arabia, and Ethiopia. His end was reached in Baku on the Caspian Sea where he was actually very painfully skinned alive. He was then beheaded.

Thomas, who we know as Doubting Thomas, did his preaching in Iraq, Iran, and India. His death came by being burned first, then speared with a javelin in Madras, India.

The lesser known James, known as James the Less probably because he was smaller than John's brother, James, was killed for his preaching in Egypt.

Jude, also known as Thaddaeus, preached in Iraq before joining Simon the Zealot in Persia (Iran) where both were beaten to death with sticks and clubs.

Simon the Zealot first preached in Egypt before he met his cruel end with Jude in Persia.

John, the brother of James, was the only one of the original eleven who died of natural causes. He preached in Turkey and Asia Minor. Of course, although he was not martyred for what he preached, he was lowered in boiling oil head first, and when he survived was banished to the Isle of Patmos in the Aegean Sea, which was like being sent to do hard labor in a prison rock quarry. It was not a resort and he was a very old man at the time.

Matthais, the one who replaced Judas, preached in Turkey before being killed in Ethiopia for his preaching by being nailed to the ground with spikes and then beheaded.

Paul, who originally persecuted the Christians himself, was often beaten, stoned, flogged, and in other ways unmercifully tortured before he eventually was beheaded in Rome.

Finally, James, the half-brother of Jesus, who thought his brother was insane when He was alive, started telling the resurrection story and was stoned to death for it, as we saw in the account by Josephus.

All fourteen were tortured for telling the story, and only one did not die at the hand of his captors because of it.

Now, let's be just the least bit realistic. Is there any way in our wildest imaginations that we could believe that these fourteen men, all but two totally alone at their deaths, undergoing the most heinous forms of torture, including being skinned alive, hundreds and thousands of miles apart from their nearest conspirator, knowing that all they had to do was recant the story to stop the torture and their own painful death, would have kept up a lie that could do no one any good at all, about a man that they knew to be a lunatic?

To believe that not a single one of them, in unheard of agony, knowing that the others would probably never find out anyway, would not have given in to the excruciating pain and said the simple words that their torturers wanted to hear, stands alone as the craziest belief possible. We could scour the planet and never find fourteen men who would go through what these men went through, totally isolated, for a meaningless hoax.

Only a real encounter with the true risen Christ could explain the reality of what happened in the lives of these men. There is no other explanation. Jesus actually arose from the grave, exactly like He said He would. There is no other possibility.

Peter stated it plainly for us when he said, *"We did not follow cleverly invented stories when we told you about the power and coming of our Lord*

Jesus Christ, but we were eyewitnesses to His majesty." 2 Peter 1:16.

We have all heard that truth is more incredible than fiction. This truth, that Jesus arose from the grave, is more than that, not just because it is so astonishing a fact, but because of what it means for you and me. God exists. The Bible is how He communicated with us. Jesus is the Son of God. And He arose from the dead. These four things we have now seen are provable. They are indisputable facts.

What we do with those undeniable facts are up to each of us.

I will tell you for a certainty that your individual life will not end when you die and leave this earthly body. There is an eternal life after death. And how you spend that eternity will depend on the decision you make now concerning whether or not you accept the gift of salvation that the death and resurrection of Jesus made available to you. Not everyone who dies will spend eternity with God. That is just as provable as the other facts that were proven in this book. Only those who accept Jesus as Lord and Savior will be in the privileged few.

You can be among those by sincerely asking Jesus right now to come into your life as your Lord. He is real, and He is waiting this very moment for you to call on Him. He will not turn you away. He loves you so very much.

About the Author and His Books

Although Bob Morley's educational background at the University of North Carolina was in psychology, his overriding passion is the study of all things pertaining to God, as is obvious in all of his books.

Unlocking God's Secrets was the culmination of over thirteen thousand hours of intensive research and study into that passion. It has been described as the most comprehensive single book about God and Christianity ever written, and is a must read for any truth seeker. Virtually every single page contains something that will cause both the novice and the scholar to say, "Wow!"

Musings from Me and My Master is an exciting collection of seventy articles that stir every emotion within the reader, and causes deep thinking as only this author can. In it can be found Biblical prophecies and shadows that may never have been seen before, along with a pleasant mixture of miracles and personal insights.

The Divine Maestro's Two Option Shadow

Biblical shadows contain truths God wants us to know. Intriguingly, however, His longest shadow has been "hiding" right out in the open, yet never before has it been mentioned in print. This fascinating book traces this awesome shadow through twists and turns in God's Word, revealing the divine truth we all need to see and understand. This book will change how you view God, the Bible, the world, and even your own life.

The Cup of The Harlot may well be the most definitive study of the true interpretation of end times prophecy as explained by the Apostle John himself to his student, Polycarp, after he had written Revelation. This book reveals how far afield we have gone by believing man's ideas about what the Revelation images could mean, rather than following the true divine interpretations that John laid out in the Apostolic Oral Teaching.

Through the Veil is an exciting book you will be unable to put down. With phenomenal miracles on virtually every page that were witnessed by nine great men and women of God, your faith will soar as never before. And as an added plus you will learn how you, too, can experience such miracles in your own daily life. As a Christian you must read this book. It is a true treasure.

All of these wonderful books, plus this one, will continue to be available from Amazon.com and other fine retailers for years to come. Don't miss out on the truths contained in each exceptional book. Every one of them will bless you as they teach you exciting nuggets never seen before, and bring you closer to the God who loves you.

Bob and his wife, Barbara, happily reside in Ormond Beach, Florida. They have four wonderful daughters and nine fabulous grandchildren.

Bob can be reached at **morley120@aol.com**.

Unsolicited Comments about Bob Morley's Books

The difference between you and the seminary professors that I sat under is that they know God academically, but are not empowered by Him. You are like those in Acts 4 who were recognized as being "with Jesus". God uses you in his writing. There is a giftedness and an empowering that was always lacking by my professors. **Pastor Dan P.**

This is the most well researched and written book I ever read. **Jim E.**

I was blown away with the detail, the wit, the easiness of reading your book. It is definitely what I call a "twicer," so much to grasp. **Randy T.**

The book will be close to my heart for the rest of my life. It changed my life. **Tom M.**

The kind of book I enjoy really digging into, gleaning nuggets of wisdom from. I'm particularly intrigued by the 332 Prophecies. **Zig Z.**

I am in awe. I am humbled. I am speechless. **Tondra B.**

I ordered several to send to friends. **AnnMarie L.**

There is so much research, etc. I can't find the words to express myself. I ordered more copies. All I can say is WOW. I am truly amazed. **Eleonor B.**

Unsolicited Comments about Bob Morley's Books

I really enjoyed the book... Could not put it down... I plan to buy several and give to family and friends as well as my church. **Pat F.**

I think it is a "WOW" and a tremendous learning tool. **Charlie C.**

This I know was truly inspired by our Lord, and I can't imagine all of the time that went in all of the research of it. **Corky G.**

What can I say but Wow. Very interesting and provocative. **Fred S.**

Wow! Excellent! Great! Overwhelming! Undeniable! **Steve R.**

This book is truly amazing! I have a friend that I grew up with that is in prison now that I'm going to send a copy of this book to. **John W.**

I am ordering 25 copies to give out to friends and pastors. **Allie M.**

Your book is wonderful. **Melodye D.**

I am giving this book to my son and praying that the Holy Spirit will use it in his life as He did in mine. **Gloria C.**

Unsolicited Comments about Bob Morley's Books

Awesome!!!!!! **Jay D**.

Your references to historic alliances elsewhere in the world and here in the United States have made me much more attentive. Perhaps it is the best time in history to be hyper-focused on God's prophecy. **Ben O**.

I love your book. It flows so nice it is hard to put down. **Kathy V**.

Your books have helped so many of us to find our way to our Savior. May you always continue to have the Holy Spirit guiding you.   T. M.

Enthralling. **Charles H**.

Your book is awesome – and I certainly believe that the Holy Spirit dictated that to you. There are really no words to describe the way the book affected me. **Sandra J**.

It is a wonderful book. **Ed C**.

Thank you for providing me with a book to answer many of my questions regarding the Word of God. **Fannie E**.

I can hardly put it down. It is incredible!!!!!! **Wanda J**.

I couldn't stop until the last word.   **Jane N.**

Unsolicited Comments about Bob Morley's Books

THANK YOU for your obedience in writing the book Unlocking God's Secrets. I have been able to do little else other than read this book since I bought it. My life with my Lord has been forever changed. My walk is permanently marked. I am stirred in a way that only the Holy Spirit can stir in my spirit. I see my purpose so clearly now and hope to be used to lead others to this truth. Thank you so very much!! **Sharron M**.

Thank you for your efforts and your faithfulness. Reading the Bible without studying it is difficult, at least for me. Your book has given me the desire to further study the Word. I now look at it as total truth with purpose in each word. I have purchased 10 more copies for two of my employees and some of my friends. I thank God for you. **Tony C**.

I have read Unlocking God's Secrets from front to back and will read it again and again and utilize it for study and confirmation. I wish I could describe how important it has been for me. I treasure this book. **C. H.**

I loved your book. Thank you for all of your research, study, and time. It is an amazing book. My eyes have been opened so much. **Gerri M**.

I am finished with the book and want everyone I know to have a chance to read it. You really have made a difference in my life. **Shirley H**.

Unsolicited Comments about Bob Morley's Books

Thank you for the incredible time it must have taken you to put this book together. **Jan H**.

I was in tears last night when I read about the twelve tribes of Israel and the cross formation they made. What a God we have the privilege of
serving. Thanks so much for the labor of love you've poured into this book. Thanks for letting the Lord use you so mightily. **Peter K**.

I'm really enjoying the content and wanted you to know that your message is true and fascinating. Thank you for your efforts. Your message is very timely in our world today. **Joyce R**.

I want to thank you so very much, from the bottom of my heart for your book. Bob, your book has taught me more than all the preachers and teachers I have ever studied with. **Ray T**.

You did a fantastic job on your research. **Ann K**.

It is important that every believer read this important work. **Pete K**.

One of the greatest books that I have ever read. I couldn't put it down. I am telling everybody about this book. It is really a "Wow" book. I am giving them for Christmas presents. **Lynda J**.

Printed in Great Britain
by Amazon

62803551R00077